THE PEOPLE'S COOKBOOK

THE
PEOPLE'S
COOKBOOK

A celebration of the nation's life through food

ANTONY WORRALL THOMPSON
& PAUL RANKIN

This book is published to accompany the UKTV television series entitled **The People's Cookbook**, which was first broadcast in 2006
Copyright © UKTV, 2007

The right of Antony Worrall Thompson and Paul Rankin to be identified as the authors of this book has been asserted in accordance with the Copyright, Designs and Patents Act 1988.

First published in 2007 by
The Infinite Ideas Company Limited
36 St Giles
Oxford, OX1 3LD
United Kingdom
www.infideas.com

A CIP catalogue record for this book is available from the British Library

ISBN 978–1–905940–37–0

Brand and product names are trademarks or registered trademarks of their respective owners.

Photographs on pages 7, 11, 17, 39, 45, 61, 67, 73, 83, 87, 93, 105, 121, 137 and 141 © Karen Thomas; food stylist Justine Pattison.

Photographs on pages 3, 25, 29, 35, 57, 63, 77, 101, 113, 115, 131, 145, 151 © Simon Smith; food stylist Jayne Cross.

Cover and text designed by Cylinder

Typeset by Cylinder

Printed in Italy

infiniteideas

UKTV Food's **The People's Cookbook** offers a snapshot of who we are and where we're from. As the only television channel in the UK dedicated to a love of good food, we are passionate about celebrating contemporary food culture through the meals we love to cook for family and friends.

A collection of recipes and food stories like no other, this is a book which boasts diverse and delicious dishes - well-deserved winners and runners-up from UKTV Food's highly acclaimed television series The People's Cookbook.

Back in spring 2007, we launched an award-winning campaign on our web site, www.uktvfood.co.uk, asking the public to share their special dishes and personal food stories with the nation. The resulting virtual feast was a huge success, providing rich pickings for our entertaining, evocative and emotionally charged television series.

Shortlisted dishes, championed by top chefs, Antony Worrall Thompson and Paul Rankin, were pitched against each other and voted for by a studio audience. Winning recipes enjoyed the accolade and honour of making it onto the pages of this very special book and our two top chefs pitched in by including their personal favourites as runners-up. As AWT reflected:

"Modern Britain is proud of its culinary culture and recipes in this book embrace global flavours, champion regional traditions, and celebrate the very best of honest home cooking..."

From Chinese-inspired curries to mums-own bakes, kebabs to British classics, African stews to saucy Italian pastas – the People's Cookbook is a celebration of our lives through food.

We like to think of this book as a culinary heirloom to hand down through generations of future home cooks and food lovers.

Paul Moreton
UKTV Food Channel Head

A WORD WITH THE CHEFS

Antony: *The number of different cultures featured in the series has been really surprising and working on this project has been illuminating. Some of these recipes stay true to tradition and use the same ingredients as would have been used abroad, but many have been adapted to incorporate local ingredients. It's great to combine British salmon with oriental elements like soy. A few dishes did sound quite bizarre at first glance – but they were actually very tasty.'*

Paul: *'Sometimes, recipes that look unpromising on paper, and maybe even in reality, turn out to have a fabulous taste.'*

Antony: *'During filming, we heard fascinating food stories. A lovely recipe for Polish beetroot soup came from someone whose grandmother had trekked across Siberia's Gobi Desert to escape Stalin's Russia. Another dish has been contributed by a survivor of the 2005 Boxing Day Tsunami. Food enables people to hang onto their cultural roots and keeps family heritage going. Although this is important everywhere, it has even more of a role in immigrant communities.'*

Paul: *'Whether people come from an immigrant background or a local one, there's an important connection made between food and family. The food we enjoy is a real connector; it cements memories.'*

Antony: *'We probably had more male finalists than I thought we'd get. When I started demonstrating cooking about five years or so ago, I might have got one man in a class; now it's about 40 per cent. I've also noticed that quite a few men insist on teaching their kids to cook.'*

Paul: *'The British palate is changing – it's becoming much more open to unfamiliar flavours.'*

Antony: *'That's been reflected in the television series. I was really glad to see akee being cooked with salt fish. I love Jamaica, and have akee for breakfast every day when I visit. I also remember the sweetly aromatic flavours of konafa – a delicious Middle-Eastern pastry. We've had unusual results with more familiar ingredients too – roast chicken cooked with Marmite was a winner – Marmite gave the chicken depth of flavour and we didn't really get a distinctive Marmitey taste once it was cooked. I enjoyed it so much that I've been cooking it at home.'*

Paul: *'It almost always seems to have been mum or grandma who influenced contestants. I've noticed a connection between different generations passing on recipes using local produce. It's satisfying to appreciate this deep connection with regional food.'*

Antony: *'Many contestants wanted to make sure we used items local to their region and some went so far as to bring their own to the studio. On the show, we've had contributors who are closely connected with the land – a pig farmer, a turkey breeder, a gamekeeper's wife – but we've also had home cooks insisting that we use a particular local type of potato. Their main reason for using regional produce involves supporting local businesses and not wanting to use ingredients that have travelled huge distances.*

'In the series, a love for stews has been demonstrated and also a passion for baking – the gingerbread cake really stands out for me because of its deliciously spicy flavour. And pies too – they're really popular; rustic food is coming back and pies are part of our heritage. Puddings are also top choices – I now make windrush-style bread and butter pudding at home.

Paul: *'There was a queen of puddings which was really nostalgic – it should definitely be revived and everyone should make it…'*

Antony: *'I'm a big meat fan and was won over by Korean beef, and baked ham with cola – the contestant's mother came from Atlanta, Georgia, the home of Coca Cola. One clear message is how important good butchers are to our lives, and how much people value them. A lot depends on having a good butcher when making a traditional Guyanese pepperpot with pig's trotters.*

Paul: *'It's been very inspiring cooking other people's food and discovering the powerful stories behind each dish. I'd say the message of* **The People's Cookbook** *is to source good ingredients and spend time preparing them, fine tuning favourite dishes until they're just right.'*

STARTERS & LIGHT BITES

WINNER

ROASTED FENNEL AND SOMERSET CIDER SOUP
BY TONY BRANDON

This particular recipe was inspired by wandering through farmers' markets during an autumn holiday in Somerset. It's rich, creamy and quite irresistible. I think I must have always been keen on doing things with food – my first memory of food is of my rusks, but unlike other two-year-olds I wasn't content with just gnawing at them. I had to mix them up in a bowl and was determined to turn them into something fancier. I'm a very keen cook, and once appeared on a Ready, Steady, Cook-style show where I ended up making my own pasta dough in only twelve minutes.

1. Preheat the oven to 200°C / gas 6. Trim the feathery leaves off the fennel and reserve some for the garnish. Trim the rest of the bulbs, top and bottom, then cut them into segments. Cut the onions into similar-sized segments.

2. Place the fennel and onion segments in a roasting tin and drizzle olive oil over the top. Scatter the lemon thyme, coriander and fennel seeds and some freshly ground black pepper over the vegetables. Put them in the oven and roast for 30–45 minutes until lightly caramelised. Remove the roasting tin from the oven and pour the cider over the vegetables. Return the tin to the oven for a further 15 minutes, or until the cider has almost all been absorbed and reduced.

3. Remove the tin from the oven and allow the vegetables to cool slightly, then spoon them and the juices into a blender or food processor and blend until smooth. Transfer all the vegetable purée to a large saucepan and stir in the stock. Bring the soup to the boil over a high heat. Reduce the heat to medium and leave the soup to simmer until reduced in volume by about one third.

4. Once the soup is a little cooler, press it through a fine sieve using a wooden spoon. Do this twice if you can. Return the soup to a clean pan, then stir in the cream and heat it gently, stirring constantly without letting it boil, until hot. Add the apple brandy just before serving; ladle the soup into warmed bowls and garnish it with a little of the chopped, feathery fennel leaves.

Ingredients
2 large fennel bulbs
   including the feathery leaves
2 large red onions
olive oil, for drizzling
1 bunch of lemon thyme sprigs
1 tbsp coriander seeds
1 tbsp fennel seeds
330 ml dry cider
1 litre vegetable stock
300 ml double cream
good glug of Somerset apple brandy
   or Calvados
black pepper

Servings: 4–6
Level of difficulty: Intermediate
Preparation time: 30 minutes
Cooking time: 1 hour 10 minutes
to 1 hour 25 minutes

Fennel and apples – a lovely marriage and a lovely soup
Antony

WINNER

FISH HEAD SOUP
BY IRENE SYKES

I think this soup may have originated with monks from St. Andrews, but despite being made with very cheap ingredients it's quite an elegant dish, and I love making something like this from such thrifty materials! I'm originally from a fishing village in Scotland, and was taught to cook by my grandmother who was employed as a cook on a large Scottish estate. I now live near Whitby, and it's perfect for using the fresh local fish – and I also think it demonstrates how people used to live, and how they have lived for generations. I like to serve this rich, creamy soup with oatcakes or good brown bread.

Ingredients
6 haddock heads
1 litre water
1 carrot, chopped
1 turnip, chopped
1 celery stick, chopped
handful of parsley stalks
50 g butter
50 g plain white flour
250 ml milk
1 egg yolk, beaten
3 tbsp double cream
salt and pepper
chopped flat-leaf parsley, to garnish

1. Rinse the fish heads thoroughly to remove all traces of blood. Put them in a pan with the water and slowly bring to the boil, skimming the surface as necessary to make a clear stock. Add the carrot, turnip, celery and parsley stalks, reduce the heat to low, partially cover the pan and leave to simmer for about 30 minutes, or until the vegetables are soft. Keep an eye on the water level and top up as necessary. Strain the resulting liquid – a good fish stock – into a bowl and discard the vegetables, parsley stalks and fish heads.

2. Melt the butter in a large pan over a medium-low heat. Sprinkle in the flour and stir for 2 minutes to cook out the raw taste. Gradually add the fish stock and milk. Bring to the boil, still stirring, and cook for a few minutes until thickened. Season with salt and pepper and remove from the heat. You can prepare the soup up to this stage in advance.

3. When you are ready to serve, reheat the soup and beat 2 tablespoons of the hot soup into the egg yolk in a small bowl. Pour this mixture into the soup, stirring until it thickens. Do not let the soup boil or the egg will scramble. When the soup has thickened, add the cream and serve straight away.

Servings: 4–6
Level of difficulty: Intermediate
Preparation time: 20 minutes
Cooking time: 40 minutes

This soup has a beautiful flavour and a lovely richness, a sort of velvetiness. I really liked it – and the idea of using the heads.
Paul

WINNER

CHICKEN SOUP

BY BERNADETTE HERMAN

Heart-warming and nurturing, this soup is very special to me. It reminds me of my mother, who passed away when I was only eight years old, and of Northern Ireland, where I grew up in County Antrim. Although I was so young, I was the eldest child so I took over much of the family cooking, and found cooking was one way to make things better. Since then I've always associated cooking with caring for people. A lot of love goes into my cooking.

1. The night before you want to make the soup, put the chicken or boiling fowl into a large, heavy-based pan and cover it with enough water to come to the level of the breastbone. Bring the water to the boil, skimming the surface as necessary. Reduce the heat to low, partially cover the pan and leave to simmer for 1–2 hours for a chicken, or up to 5 hours for a boiling fowl, until the flesh is tender when you pierce it with a knife or fork. Keep an eye on the water level and top up as necessary.

2. Remove the pan from the heat and leave to cool. When the bird is cool enough to handle, remove it from the liquid and set aside. Strain the liquid through a fine sieve into a large bowl and leave to cool completely, then cover with cling film and chill overnight. Remove any skin and bones from the bird and discard as well. Cut the chicken meat into bite-sized pieces, cover and put in the fridge.

3. The following day, remove the layer of fat that will have formed on the surface of the stock and discard. Pour the stock into a large saucepan and bring to just below boiling point over a high heat. Reduce the heat to low, add the leeks, onion, parsnips, carrots, most of the parsley and season to taste. Leave the soup to simmer for 30 minutes, or until the vegetables are tender. Just before the vegetables finish cooking, add the chicken to the pan and heat through. Stir in the remaining parsley and season with salt and pepper.

4. Meanwhile, bring a separate pan of salted water to the boil. Add the potatoes and boil for 15–20 minutes until they are tender. Drain well, then set aside and keep warm.

5. When you're ready to serve, divide the potatoes between soup bowls and ladle the hot soup over.

Ingredients
1 chicken or boiling fowl
2 leeks, coarsely chopped and rinsed
1 large onion, coarsely chopped
2 parsnips, coarsely chopped
3–4 carrots, coarsely chopped
1 large bunch of curly parsley, coarsely chopped
2.25 kg potatoes, peeled and cut into chunks
salt and pepper

This soup is a great old-fashioned recipe. It's important to take your time and do things like make the stock to get the best possible flavour.
Paul

Servings: 6–8
Level of difficulty: Easy
Preparation time: 20 minutes
Cooking time: Up to 5 hours, plus 45 minutes

WINNER

POLISH BEETROOT SOUP WITH DUMPLINGS (BARSZCZ)

BY ROB ELLIOT

This gloriously red soup is important and significant to me because it's the first of twelve courses in the traditional Polish supper on Christmas Eve, and because I learned it from my Polish mother. My whole life has been influenced by food. I was born in Africa with parents of two different nationalities – my father is English – so I've grown up under many different influences.

1. First put the dried mushrooms for the dumplings into enough hot water to cover and leave to soak. Now begin the soup: put the beetroot into a saucepan with the carrot, celery, onion, cabbage, dried mushroom pieces, bay leaves, parsley and water to cover. Bring it to the boil over a high heat, then reduce the heat, partially cover the pan and simmer gently for about an hour.

2. Meanwhile, make the dumplings. Sift the flour into a large bowl and season with salt and pepper to taste. Make a well in the centre and add the egg and water. Mix thoroughly and then knead the resulting dough by hand until smooth; wrap it in cling film and set aside while you make the filling.

3. The dried mushrooms for the dumpling filling should by now be fully rehydrated. Strain them, reserving the liquid and chop very finely. Melt the butter in a large saucepan over a medium heat. Add the fresh mushrooms and shallot and fry for about 3 minutes, stirring, until the shallot begins to colour. Add the rehydrated mushrooms and their liquid, turn up the heat and cook, stirring, until most of the liquid evaporates. Stir in the dill and the breadcrumbs. Take the pan off the heat.

4. Now divide the dough into eight pieces and roll out each one very thinly on a lightly floured surface. Cut the sheet of dough into 5 cm squares. Taking one square at a time, place a teaspoonful of the filling in the centre and fold the square up and over it, making a triangle. Crimp the edges together. Then fold the two corners of the longest edge inwards so that they overlap, and crimp them together too. Set each one aside on a floured board while you make the rest.

5. Bring a large pan of salted water to the boil over a high heat. Gently add the dumplings, stirring gently to prevent them sticking to each other. Bring the water back to the boil and simmer for about 3 minutes, or until they float to the surface.

6. Strain the soup into a bowl and discard the vegetables. Reheat the soup in the rinsed pan until hot, then add a little vinegar to taste: this gives it a sharp edge without masking the sweetness of the beetroot. Adjust the seasoning if necessary. Use a slotted spoon to remove the dumplings from the hot water, then add them to the soup and serve.

Ingredients

4 beetroot, peeled and cut into
   julienne strips
1 carrot, cut into chunks
2 sticks of celery, sliced
1 large onion, sliced
3 cabbage leaves, roughly sliced
4 large pieces of dried mushrooms
2 bay leaves
2 large sprigs of flat-leaf parsley
splash of cider or perry vinegar

For the dumplings:
2 dried mushrooms
100 g plain flour, plus extra for dusting
1 egg, beaten
1 tbsp water
1 tsp butter
4 fresh brown button mushrooms,
   chopped
1 large shallot, chopped
1 tbsp chopped dill
1 tbsp dried breadcrumbs
salt and pepper

Servings: 3–4
Level of difficulty: Intermediate
Preparation time: 20 minutes
Cooking time: 1 hour

Calling this simply 'beetroot soup' doesn't give it the glamour it deserves. It's magical.
Antony

WINNER

MEATBALL AND LOVAGE SOUP (CIORBA DI PERISOARA)
BY FRANCES JONES-DAVIES

I think this traditional Turkish recipe is far healthier than the sort of 'special' food for children you find in the UK. I grew up in Sudan and loved the food there, so much so that I was often found after supper eating the marrow from the thrown-out bones with the beggars. When I came to the UK at the age of six, I really didn't like the food but didn't start cooking until much later, when I moved to Turkey with my husband and cooked with the village women. Their children ate the same as the adults, though often in soup form such as this dish.

Ingredients
For the meatballs:
1 tbsp olive oil
1 onion, finely chopped
450 g lean minced beef
small bunch of lovage, finely chopped
2 tbsp ground rice
1 free range egg, beaten
5 drops of Tabasco sauce
salt and pepper

For the soup:
2 tbsp olive oil
1 onion, finely chopped
1 large carrot, finely chopped
1 celery stick, finely chopped
1.5 litres of water
3 tbsp tomato purée
2 beef stock cubes (preferably organic)
100 ml white wine vinegar
1 tsp granulated sugar
small bunch of lovage, leaves only,
  roughly chopped
salt and pepper

1. Make the meatballs first. Heat the oil in a small frying pan over a medium-low heat. Add the onion and fry, stirring frequently, for about 10 minutes until it is transparent. Put it in a large mixing bowl with the minced beef, lovage, ground rice, egg and Tabasco, and season with salt and pepper to taste. Mix everything together, kneading the mixture against the side of the bowl until you can feel the consistency become smooth and almost dough-like.

2. Line a baking sheet with greaseproof paper or baking parchment. Take a small amount of the meat mixture, about the size of a hazelnut, and roll it into a ball between your hands. Put it on the baking sheet and repeat with the rest of the mixture, then set aside. It is handy to have a bowl of warm water beside you; dip your hands in every few minutes to stop the meatballs sticking to your palms.

3. Now make the soup. In a large pan, heat the olive oil over a low heat. Add the onion, carrot and celery and fry gently, stirring frequently, for 10 minutes. Pour in the water, increase the heat to medium, and simmer for 5 minutes. Add the tomato purée, crumbled stock cubes, vinegar and sugar and simmer for another 15 minutes. Gently add the meatballs to the soup, reduce the heat to low, partially cover the pan and continue cooking for 30 minutes. Stir in the lovage and season with salt and pepper. Leave the soup to simmer for 10 minutes longer, before serving hot.

Servings: 6–8
Level of difficulty: Easy
Preparation time: 20 minutes
Cooking time: 1 hour 20 minutes

Delicious; exotic and rustic at the same time. It's well worth trying; if you can't find lovage, use celery leaves.
Paul

WINNER

SPINACH AND LENTIL SOUP (RISHTA)

BY PATRICIA KATEB

Inexpensive and very easy to make, this filling soup can easily be enjoyed by vegetarians by substituting vegetable stock for the chicken Bovril. I grew up in Alexandria, where I met my husband. My father is British and my mother Lebanese. My grandmother taught me to cook and this is a very traditional dish which I still like making today for my own family. Now I'm retired and my two children are working, I spend a lot of time looking after my grandchildren when they finish school – which I love – and I really enjoy cooking with them. I don't approve of fast food; I'm a big believer in the importance of people sitting down together to appreciate a properly cooked meal.

Ingredients

100 g dried brown lentils
5 garlic cloves, peeled
75 g fresh coriander, leaves and stems
3 tbsp sunflower oil
1 tbsp ground coriander
2 tsp chicken Bovril
1 litre boiling water
½ tsp salt, or to taste
200 g fresh spinach leaves,
  finely chopped
40 g mini pasta shapes
salt

1. Place the lentils in a bowl, cover with cold water, and leave to soak for 30 minutes. Meanwhile put the garlic and coriander leaves and stems in a food processor or liquidiser and process to a paste. (Or use a pestle and mortar and pound them to a paste.)

2. Heat the oil in a large heavy-based saucepan over a medium heat. Add the garlic and coriander paste and sauté until it is browned all over. Stir in the ground coriander.

3. Add the chicken Bovril to the pan along with the boiling water and stir to dissolve. Drain the soaked lentils, add them to the pan and stir everything together. Bring to the boil then reduce the heat, cover the pan and simmer for about 35 minutes until the lentils are tender. Season to taste with the salt. Add the spinach and pasta, then bring the mixture back to the boil. Cover the pan, reduce the heat and simmer for a further 15 minutes, or until the pasta is tender. Ladle the soup into warmed bowls to serve.

Servings: 4
Level of difficulty: Easy
Preparation time: 15 minutes,
plus 30 minutes soaking time
Cooking time: About 1 hour 5 minutes

A stunner. It's delicious and it's fine with frozen spinach, too. Many people asked for this recipe at the recording: a great sign!
Paul

ANTONY'S CHOICE

PARSNIP AND CARROT SOUP (TRECAWL)

BY NICK JENKINS

1. Heat the oil in a large saucepan over a medium heat. Add the onions and garlic and fry, stirring frequently, for about 5 minutes until soft. Add the carrots and parsnips and fry for a further 5 minutes. Stir in the tinned tomatoes and passata and bring the mixture to the boil. Then reduce the heat to low, partially cover the pan, and simmer for about 30 minutes, or until the vegetables are tender.

2. Add the soy sauce, stock cubes, mustard and herbs and remove the pan from the heat. Leave the soup to cool slightly, then process it in a food processor or liquidiser until coarsely puréed. Return the soup to the pan and reheat. Ladle the soup into warmed bowls and serve with a sprinkling of parsley and grated cheese. Accompany with a hunk of granary bread.

Ingredients

2 tbsp olive oil
3 large onions, roughly chopped
2 garlic cloves, sliced
6 large carrots, roughly chopped
6 large parsnips, roughly chopped
4 x 420g tins of tomatoes
500 ml passata
2 tsp soy sauce
2 vegetable stock cubes, crumbled
2 tsp English mustard
1–2 tsp dried mixed herbs, to taste
chopped fresh parsley
grated cheese, to garnish
granary bread, to serve

Servings: 8
Level of difficulty: Easy
Preparation time: 10 minutes
Cooking time: 40 minutes

This tasty soup would be wonderful on a cold winter's night, and it's good value too.
Antony

JOE GREY SOUP
BY PAULA STANFORD

Made with chipolata sausages and unsmoked bacon, this hearty soup is more like a stew than a broth. It's very easy to make and filling too.

1. Heat the oil in a large, deep frying pan. Add the sausages to the pan and fry, turning frequently, for 8–10 minutes, or until browned. Remove them from the pan and cut each one into three pieces, then return them to the pan. Add the bacon and continue frying until the pieces are browned. Stir in the onions and cook until browned.

2. Cover the contents of the pan with boiling water, but don't fill it to the top. Add the potatoes and reduce the heat to a simmer and continue cooking until they are tender; you may need to top up the liquid with more boiling water.

3. Add the tomatoes and crumble the stock cubes into the pan. Stir well and continue simmering until the tomatoes are soft. Serve on plates rather than in bowls, and accompany with lots of chunky bread and butter.

Ingredients

1 tbsp vegetable oil
8 pork chipolata sausages
8 rindless rashers of unsmoked
  back bacon, each cut into 3 pieces
2 onions, cut into large chunks
5 potatoes, sliced
5 tomatoes, sliced
3 beef stock cubes
chunky brown bread and butter, to serve

This is an old gypsy dish, and I love the big chunks of potatoes in it. The result is greater than the sum of its parts!
Paul

Servings: 6
Level of difficulty: Easy
Preparation time: 10 minutes
Cooking time: About 45 minutes

PAUL'S CHOICE

CRAB THERMIDOR
BY CARLA LAGAN-BROWN

This luxurious starter is one to consider when you want something special for a dinner party. You can prepare the creamy crab mixture several hours in advance and keep it refrigerated until quickly finishing off under the grill just before your guests sit down at the table. If you prefer something more substantial, say for lunch, add boiled new potatoes and dressed mixed salad leaves.

Ingredients
135 g butter
2 onions, chopped
200 g fresh white breadcrumbs
  (made by whizzing slices of one-or two-
  day old bread in a blender)
35 g plain white flour
90 ml full-fat milk
175 g clotted cream
225 g small cooked and peeled prawns
450 g cooked white crab meat
50 g Parmesan cheese, freshly grated
salt and pepper

1. Melt 75 g of the butter in a large frying pan over a very low heat. Add the onions and fry, stirring frequently, for 20–30 minutes until they are really soft, but not browned. Meanwhile, melt the remaining butter in another frying pan over a low heat. Add the breadcrumbs and fry, turning occasionally, until they are golden brown. Remove them from the heat and put to one side.

2. When the onions are ready, stir in the flour and cook gently for 1 minute, stirring. Remove the pan from the heat and gradually stir in the milk, then return the pan to the heat and cook for 1–2 minutes until the mixture thickens, still stirring. Remove the pan from the heat again and add the clotted cream, mixing well, then season with salt and a little pepper. Add the prawns and crab meat and mix them in gently so that some pieces of crab remain intact.

3. Preheat the grill to medium-hot. Spoon the crab mixture into 6 clean scallop shells or individual heatproof serving dishes. Sprinkle each one with fried breadcrumbs, followed by a good sprinkling of Parmesan. Place them under the grill for a minute or so until the cheese has melted, then serve straight away.

Servings: 6
Level of difficulty: Easy
Preparation time: 15 minutes
Cooking time: 35–45 minutes

Great, with lots of crab. It's also worth trying this recipe using only prawns – or perhaps mixed seafood.
Paul

ANTONY'S CHOICE

COQUILLES ST JACQUES
BY NIGEL COOK

The scallops are quickly cooked in this classic French recipe so they remain tender and succulent. This stylish dish can be served on its own or you can add slices of French bread to mop up the delicious cooking juices.

1. Preheat the grill to medium. Heat the oil or melt the butter in a medium-sized pan over a medium heat. Add the onion and garlic and fry, stirring, for 2–3 minutes until softened and translucent. Add the parsley and season with salt and pepper. Remove the mixture from the pan with a slotted spoon and set aside, leaving any juices behind.

2. Reheat the juices in the pan. When they are very hot, add the scallops and cook them for 20–40 seconds on each side until golden. Return the garlic and onion to the pan, followed by the white wine, and cook rapidly for 1–2 minutes until the liquid is reduced. Stir in the double cream and cook steadily until further reduced and thickened.

3. Spoon the scallop mixture into a flameproof dish and cover with grated cheese. Place the dish under the grill until the cheese is golden. Garnish with parsley and serve immediately.

Ingredients

1 tbsp olive oil or 15 g butter
½ onion, finely chopped
2 garlic cloves, crushed
a medium handful of fresh parsley
8 scallops, off the shell
125 ml Chardonnay
150–160 ml double cream
good handful of mixed grated cheese
 (¼ Parmesan, ¾ mature Cheddar)
sprigs of parsley, to garnish.
salt and pepper

Coquilles St Jacques is a classic and it's a delicious dish, quite sophisticated.
Antony

Servings: 2
Level of difficulty: Easy
Preparation time: 15 minutes
Cooking time: 15 minutes

WINNER

SALT FISH WITH AKEE

BY CATHERINE DYER

You'll find canned akee, also spelt ackee, in Caribbean markets and some supermarkets. Thin, brittle pieces of salt fish are readily available in Caribbean and Mediterranean food shops, as well as from some fishmongers. I think this is particularly good served with roasted breadfruit, another Jamaican favourite, and boiled white rice. This quick and easy recipe with a touch of spicy heat, is the national dish of Jamaica, though everyone has their own way of cooking it, and it reminds me of my roots. My parents came to Britain from Jamaica in the 1960s, and at first they couldn't find the ingredients to make the food that they loved so much. I grew up in London, listening to stories about life back home – there were always loads of people in the house as my mother loved cooking and entertaining – and I gradually learned to make the traditional Afro-Caribbean dishes that were so important to them.

Ingredients
3 tbsp vegetable oil
1 red onion, chopped
1 red pepper, cored, deseeded
   and chopped
3 spring onions, chopped
2 medium tomatoes, chopped
½ Scotch bonnet chilli, deseeded
   and chopped
400 g salt cod, soaked in several
   changes of water over night
540 g can of akee, drained and rinsed
1 tsp chopped fresh thyme
black pepper

1. Heat the oil in a large frying pan over a medium-high heat. Add the red onion, red pepper, spring onions, tomatoes and chilli and fry, stirring, for about 5 minutes, or until the onion and pepper are soft.

2. Drain the salted fish, discarding the soaking water, and add it to the pan along with the akee. Continue stirring for about 5 minutes, or until the fish is tender and flakes easily. Season it with a little black pepper and stir in the thyme, before serving.

I love akee, and I really think anyone who hasn't tasted it should give it a try.
Antony

Servings: 4
Level of difficulty: Easy
Preparation time: 15 minutes
Cooking time: About 10 minutes

WINNER

MAURITIAN PRAWN CURRY
BY NICOLA CLARKE

This dish reminds me of my roots in Africa and of my family… I think that no matter where you are, food immediately takes you back to the people and places you miss. I was born and brought up in Zimbabwe, but my grandmother was from Mauritius and her family's cook taught my grandfather to make this dish. It's been passed on and is now made by his relatives all over the world. Mauritius is a real melting pot of different cultures; it's been a colony for various European nations and there are a lot of African and Indian influences too. I like to serve it with boiled white rice and poppadums, accompanied by a fruit chutney, green mango or lemon pickle, and raisins.

1. Preheat the oven to 180°C / gas 4, and heat the oil in a flameproof casserole over a medium heat. Add the onions and aubergine to the casserole and fry for 10 minutes, stirring occasionally, until softened. Add the tomatoes and cook for a further 2–3 minutes. Add all of the remaining ingredients except the prawns and lime juice, and bring the mixture to the boil. Add a little water if the sauce is too thick.

2. Place the prawns in a bowl and cover them with half the lime juice to marinate them. Cover the casserole, reduce the heat to low and leave the curry to simmer for 10 minutes, then stir in the marinated prawns and the remaining lime juice. Stir well to coat the prawns in the sauce, cover the casserole again, place in the oven and cook for 30 minutes. Serve hot.

Ingredients
2 tbsp vegetable oil
2 onions, finely chopped
1 aubergine, roughly chopped
  into 3 cm pieces
400 g tin of chopped tomatoes
1 tbsp soy sauce
1 tbsp Worcester sauce
1 tbsp sweet mango chutney
1 tbsp white wine vinegar
1 tbsp granulated sugar
1 tbsp raisins
3 bay leaves
1 tsp paprika
1 tsp onion salt
1 tsp celery salt
½ tsp dried mixed herbs
½ tsp turmeric
½ tsp ground ginger
1 tbsp curry powder
1 tsp mixed spice
500 g raw king prawns
juice of 1 lime

A good, interesting curry with exquisite flavours.
Antony

Servings: 4
Level of difficulty: Easy
Preparation time: 15 minutes
Cooking time: About 1 hour

PAUL'S CHOICE

CULLEN SPINK
BY BOB SPINK

This is a personal variation of a Scottish favourite, originating from Cullen, on the coast of the Moray Firth in Scotland. The golden Arbroath smokies, or simply smokies, take on their distinctive colour and flavour by being slowly smoked over hardwood. Thickened with potatoes and enriched with cream, this is versatile enough to serve as a first course or a simple meal with just some crusty bread.

1. Place the flaked smokies in a medium-sized pan with the water and gently bring to the boil, then immediately remove the pan from the heat and set aside. After 10 minutes lift the fish from the water using a slotted spoon but don't break the flakes up further. Set them aside.

2. Strain the cooking liquid through a fine sieve into a clean pan. Add the onions, potatoes, turmeric and cayenne pepper. Cover the pan and simmer over a medium heat for 20–25 minutes until the potatoes are tender. Remove the pan from the heat and mash the potatoes, onions and cooking liquid together, using a potato masher. Once thoroughly combined, add the milk slowly, stirring constantly, until the liquid is blended with the potato mixture.

3. Return the pan to a low heat, and add the flaked smokies and butter. Stirring gently, cook the mixture until it is hot but do not allow it to boil. Taste and add salt if necessary – but remember that smoked fish already contains salt so you might not need any. Pour the soup into warmed bowls, swirl cream in the centre of each one and garnish with a little parsley before serving.

Ingredients

1 pair of Arbroath smokies, flaked
300 ml water
2 onions, finely chopped
3 large potatoes, peeled and thinly sliced
¼ tsp ground turmeric
pinch of cayenne pepper
450 ml milk
1 tbsp butter
salt ,optional
3–4 tbsp double cream
chopped fresh parsley, to garnish

This is an individual take on a Scottish classic, a proper hearty broth. It's five star, too.
Paul

Servings: 3–4
Level of difficulty: easy
Preparation time: 20 minutes
Cooking time: 40 minutes

WINNER

MOLLY MALONE CROUTON POT
BY NEELIA HUTCHINS

You'll notice a taste of Spain in this fish and shellfish feast served with piped mashed potatoes. The inspiration for this filling dish comes from the time my husband Dennis and I ran a bistro in Spain. Now, however, I make it regularly at the Age Concern Alice Cross Community Centre, in Teignmouth, where I'm the caterer. In 2005 I was a runner-up as Radio 4's dinner lady of the year. But when I first met Dennis – I've been married to him for 52 years – I wasn't a good cook; the first thing I made for him was a vegetable casserole, and all the vegetables were raw!

Ingredients

1 kg potatoes, cut into chunks
350 ml milk
330 g skinless cod fillet
175 g rock salmon or huss fillet
200 ml dry white wine
24 large mussels in the shell, cleaned
110 g fresh cockles, shelled
30 g butter
2 onions, finely chopped
4 garlic cloves, finely chopped
½ red pepper, cored, deseeded
  and finely chopped
30 g plain white flour
4 tsp tomato ketchup
2 tsp chopped fresh dill
2 tsp chopped fresh parsley
2 medium slices of white bread,
salt and pepper
a little sunflower oil, for frying
dressed mixed salad leaves, to serve

1. Preheat the oven to 150°C / gas 2. Discard any cracked mussels or open ones that do not snap closed when tapped. Cook the potatoes in a pan of boiling salted water for 15–20 minutes until tender, then drain them well. Return them to the pan and mash until smooth, then add half the milk and mix it in. Cool the mashed potatoes slightly, then pipe the creamy potatoes in a ring around the edge of 4 individual ovenproof serving dishes. Put them in the low oven to keep warm.

2. Meanwhile, place the cod and rock salmon in a large pan. Pour the wine into the pan and bring it gently to the boil, then reduce the heat and simmer for 3–4 minutes until the fish is almost cooked. Add the mussels and cockles and simmer for 3–4 minutes until the mussels have opened (discard any unopened ones). Strain the liquor off the fish and reserve it separately; keep the fish warm.

3. Melt the butter in another pan over medium heat. Add the onions, garlic and red pepper and sauté them for 5 minutes, or until softened. Stir in the flour and cook for 1 minute, stirring. Remove the pan from the heat and gradually add the remaining milk, stirring constantly, then stir in the reserved fish liquor. Return to the heat and cook the sauce, stirring, until it is thickened and smooth. Simmer it gently for 2 minutes and stir in the tomato ketchup.

4. Flake the cod and rock salmon and remove 16 of the mussels from their shells (discard the shells). Add the flaked fish, shelled mussels and cockles to the sauce. Stir in the chopped dill and parsley, and salt and pepper to taste. Cover the mixture and keep it hot.

5. Using a 5 cm pastry cutter, cut 8 rounds from the bread slices. Heat a little sunflower oil in a frying pan over a medium-high heat. Add the bread rounds and fry (in two batches, if necessary) until golden and crisp on both sides, turning once. Drain them on kitchen paper.

6. Arrange the salad leaves on 4 serving platters. Remove the dishes with the piped potato rings from the oven and spoon some fish sauce into the centre of each potato ring, then garnish each serving with 2 mussels in their shells and 2 crisp croutons. Serve on the platters accompanied by a salad garnish.

Servings: 4
Level of difficulty: Intermediate
Preparation time: 35 minutes
Cooking time: 40 minutes

It's interesting to see a variety of fish and
shellfish being used in a single dish like this.
Antony

PAUL'S CHOICE

SALMON KEDGEREE
BY CAROLYN CHESSHIRE

1. Pour the stock into a small pan and bring to the boil. Reduce the heat and then leave it just simmering over a low heat to keep hot.

2. Melt half the butter in a heavy-based, flameproof casserole over a medium heat. Add the shallots and fry, stirring, for 2 minutes, or until they are beginning to soften. Add the mushrooms and cook for another minute.

3. Rinse the basmati rice under running water until the water runs clear, then add to the casserole. Stir well to ensure the rice is coated with the butter, and cook for another minute. Pour the hot stock into the casserole and bring it to the boil, then reduce the heat to low. Cover the casserole and leave the rice to simmer for 10–15 minutes, stirring occasionally, until the grains of rice are soft and separated and all the liquid has been absorbed.

4. Gently stir in the cream and most of the herbs, before gently folding in the salmon and eggs to heat them through. Add the remaining butter, a little at a time, until the mix is even more creamy – you may not need it all. Season the kedgeree to taste, and then remove it from the heat. Sprinkle over a few more chopped herbs before serving.

Ingredients
600 ml chicken stock
150 g butter
6 shallots, halved lengthways
125 g button mushrooms,
  wiped and sliced
275 g organic basmati rice
50 ml organic double cream
small bunch of dill, chopped
small bunch of flat-leaf parsley, chopped
225 g cooked organic salmon, flaked
8 quail eggs, soft-boiled, shelled
  and halved
salt and pepper

Servings: 6
Level of difficulty: Easy
Preparation time: 10 minutes
Cooking time: 25 minutes

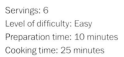

This is a lovely light version of kedgeree which was very unlucky not to win; it's a delicious recipe.
Paul

PAUL'S CHOICE

FUSION-STYLE WEST COAST SALMON
BY DR RHYS EVANS

1. Prepare the teriyaki sauce. Put the soy sauce and vinegar in a small saucepan over a high heat and bring to the boil. Add the sugar and sesame oil and stir until the sugar dissolves. Put the ginger in a piece of cloth and squeeze the juice straight into the pan, then add the chilli sauce. Discard the ginger in the cloth.

2. Once the sauce is boiling, turn the heat down and leave to simmer for 15–20 minutes, stirring frequently, until it is reduced by half. As it boils down it will thicken and the surface will be covered with fairly large bubbles (up to 3 mm in diameter). If it is slow to respond, add a bit more sesame oil. It is ready when the sauce has thickened to coating consistency. Lay the salmon flat in a dish, then pour over the warm sauce. Turn the salmon over so both sides are well coated, then set aside and leave to marinate for an hour at room temperature.

3. Preheat the grill to medium. Place the salmon on the grill rack, skin side up, and brush with some of the teriyaki sauce remaining in the dish. Position the rack about 10 cm from the source of heat and grill for 5–10 minutes. Using a fish slice or two spatulas gently turn the fish over and brush with the remaining sauce. Continue grilling for a further 5 minutes, or until the fish is cooked through when you test it with a knife and the flesh flakes easily. Let the salmon sit for 5 minutes then serve with a little wasabi.

Ingredients

For the teriyaki sauce:
250 ml dark soy sauce
250 ml seasoned Japanese rice vinegar
6 tbsp golden caster sugar
2 tbsp sesame oil
4 cm piece of fresh ginger, peeled
   and finely grated
2 tbsp sweet chilli sauce

For the fish:
3 kg side of organic salmon, skin on
vegetable oil for the grill rack
prepared wasabi, to serve

This was so unlucky not to win. You should definitely try this if you enjoy clean, oriental, fish tastes.
Paul

Servings: 12
Level of difficulty: Intermediate
Preparation time: 5 minutes, plus 1 hour marinating
Cooking time: About 40 minutes

WINNER

AROMATIC CHILLI SALMON
BY LIN MCKENZIE

East meets West in this complete meal on a plate made with tender salmon fillets, crisp stir-fried courgettes and garlicky broccoli. I'm originally from Shanxi Province in China, but I've been in Edinburgh for eight years, where I live with my husband and daughter. I love living in Scotland but sometimes it's difficult to find traditional Chinese ingredients, so I have learned to use local ones instead – my mother would have used river carp for this recipe. She worked full time when I was growing up, so I've been cooking since I was eight years old. This dish brings lots of happy memories of my childhood and family in China, but also of my new life, and my new family, in Scotland.

Ingredients
3 x 175 g salmon fillets
150–175 ml whisky
5 tbsp light soy sauce
pinch of white pepper
2 tbsp vegetable oil
little plain white flour, for dusting

For the sauce:
1 tbsp Chinese or Korean chilli paste
5 tbsp whisky
2 spring onions, sliced into 3 cm lengths
4 thin slices of fresh ginger,
  peeled and chopped
1 tsp sesame oil
1 tbsp clear honey
3 tbsp hot water

For the courgettes:
2 tbsp oil
2 garlic cloves, finely chopped
3 courgettes, peeled and diced
light soy sauce, to taste
chopped spring onion, to garnish

For the garlic broccoli:
500 g broccoli, separated into florets
4–5 tbsp oil
2 garlic cloves, finely chopped
3 tbsp light soy sauce

Servings: 3
Level of difficulty: Easy
Preparation time: 30 minutes,
plus at least 2 hours marinating
Cooking time: 25 minutes

1. Place the fillets in a dish large enough to hold the fillets in a single layer. Combine the whisky, soy sauce and white pepper and pour over the salmon. Cover the dish and chill for at least 2 hours; don't leave it longer than half a day.

2. Take the fish out of the fridge and heat the oil in a large frying pan with a lid over a medium-high heat. Lift the fillets out of the marinade, pat them dry and dust them with flour. Put the fillets in the pan, flesh side down, and fry for about 2 minutes, or until they are golden. Combine all the sauce ingredients – the chilli paste, whisky, spring onions, ginger, sesame oil, honey and hot water – and pour it over the fish. Cover the pan, reduce the heat to medium-low and leave the fillets to simmer for 4–6 minutes until the sauce is reduced and sticky.

3. Prepare the vegetables, starting with the courgettes. Heat the oil in a frying pan over a high heat until it's really hot. Add the garlic and courgettes and stir-fry for 3–4 minutes. Add the light soy sauce and cook for another 2 minutes, or until tender. Sprinkle with a little spring onion.

4. Bring a pan of water to the boil over a high heat. Add the broccoli, reduce the heat and simmer for 2–3 minutes until soft, then drain thoroughly. Heat the oil in another pan over a high heat. Add the garlic and stir-fry for about 30 seconds. Tip this into the broccoli, along with the soy sauce. Serve the salmon and vegetables with steamed rice.

Scotland meets China, and it's got a good balance of all the flavours; they're just in perfect harmony.
Antony

ANTONY'S CHOICE

MEAT SAMOSAS
BY ALYA RAFIQ

Ingredients

450 g minced lamb
2 onions, plus 1 small onion, chopped
5 garlic cloves, finely chopped
7.5 cm piece of fresh ginger, peeled
    and finely grated
2 tsp garam masala
1 tsp cumin seeds
2 long green chillies, deseeded
    and finely chopped
1 tsp dried chilli flakes
1 tsp hot chilli powder
1 tsp salt, plus extra for boiling
    the potatoes
225 g Maris Piper potatoes, diced
125 g frozen peas, defrosted
bunch of coriander, finely chopped
vegetable oil, for deep frying

For the pastry:
500 g plain white flour, plus extra
    for dusting
1 tbsp sunflower oil
1 tsp salt
about 500 ml water

For the paste:
6–8 tbsp water
2 tbsp plain flour

Servings: Makes 32
Level of difficulty: Intermediate
Preparation time: 1 hour
Cooking time: 20 minutes, plus deep-frying.

1. Put the mince in a large pan over a high heat along with the 2 onions and the garlic, ginger, spices, chillies, chilli flakes, chilli powder and salt. Cover the pan and cook for 15 minutes, stirring occasionally, or until all the meat juices have been absorbed.

2. Meanwhile, bring a large pan of salted water to the boil over a high heat. Add the potatoes and boil for 10–15minutes until just tender. Drain them well and add them, together with the peas, to the meat. Cook this filling mixture over a medium heat for 3 minutes, then remove the pan from the heat and leave it to cool. Once the mixture has cooled, stir in the small onion and coriander.

3. While the filling mixture is cooling, make the pastry. Combine the flour, oil and salt in a bowl and make a well in the centre. Add enough of the water to make a pastry dough and knead it well in the bowl until smooth. Using your hands, shape the pastry into 8 balls, about 5 cm in diameter, and leave them to rest for 10 minutes, covered with a cloth.

4. Roll each ball out on a lightly floured surface into a thin circle about 10 cm across. Cut the circle into quarters then pile all of the quarters up, with a sprinkling of flour between the layers so that they don't stick – set aside. To make the paste, stir the water into the flour until it is the consistency of single cream.

5. Take one piece of the pastry and brush a little of the paste along the curved edge. Shape the pastry into a cone, folding it and sealing the curved sides together so that you have one open side. Fill the samosa with a dessertspoonful of the cooled meat mixture and, using your fingers, moisten the open edges of the samosa pastry with more flour-and-water paste. Seal the pastry together over the meat so that you have a triangular package. Set aside and repeat the process with the remaining pastry.

6. Heat enough oil for deep-frying in a deep-fat fryer or heavy-based saucepan until it reaches 180°–190°C, or a cube of bread browns in 60 seconds. Add the samosas in batches and fry them for 5–6 minutes until golden, then remove with a slotted spoon and place on a plate lined with kitchen paper. Keep them warm in a low oven while you fry the remaining samosas.

You might think doing these would be fiddly, but Alya uses a great technique for rolling the dough and filling the samosas.
Antony

WINNER

SPICED BEEF KEBABS WITH MINT AND CORIANDER CHUTNEY
BY SUNEIL KHER

These spicy kebabs and fresh-tasting chutney are ideal for entertaining, because so much of the work can be done in advance. My parents left India after partition and ended up in Northern Ireland, where they were among the first Indian immigrants. I was born here, but I have a great affection for the cooking of Northern India – my parents came from the Punjab. My father taught me this dish, and it brings back memories of my parents. I've travelled widely as a restaurant manager, working in both New York and India, but now I'm a voluntary worker, chairing a multicultural forum hoping to ease any problems ethnic minorities may face. I firmly believe that food can bring different cultures together. My choice of accompaniments for this are naan breads, a salad and a bowl of yogurt.

1. Start by preparing the kebabs. Blend the onion in a mini food processor to a smooth paste and then put it in a large bowl along with the beef, coriander, ginger, garlic paste, chillies, cumin, ajwain seeds and salt. Mix everything well until thoroughly combined, then cover the bowl and chill it for 30 minutes.

2. Divide the chilled mixture into 12 pieces and form each portion into a sausage shape. Heat the olive oil in a frying pan over a medium-high heat. Add the kebabs and fry until browned on all sides. Add the water, turn the heat to low, cover the pan and cook for a further 20 minutes, or until they are browned and tender.

3. Meanwhile make the chutney. Put the coriander, mint and onion in a blender and process until they are roughly chopped. Add the olive oil, mango powder, pomegranate powder, sugar, lime juice, vinegar and green chillies and blend again until you have a smooth paste. Add enough water to give a pouring consistency, then transfer the chutney into a bowl. Cover and chill in the fridge while the kebabs finish cooking.

4. Once the kebabs are nicely browned, serve them straight away with the mint and coriander chutney.

Ingredients

For the kebabs:
1 medium onion, finely chopped
500 g lean minced beef
small bunch of fresh coriander, finely chopped
5 cm piece of fresh ginger, peeled and finely grated
1 tbsp garlic paste
2 green chillies
2 tsp ground cumin
2 tsp ajwain seeds (carom seed, available from Indian shops)
1 tbsp salt
2–3 tbsp olive oil
150 ml water

For the chutney:
100 g fresh coriander
100 g fresh mint
1 small onion, finely chopped
2 tbsp olive oil
25 g mango powder (available from Indian shops)
25 g pomegranate powder (available from Indian shops)
3 tsp sugar
juice of 1 lime
40 ml white wine vinegar
2 green chillies, finely chopped
about 30 ml water

Servings: 4
Level of difficulty: Easy
Preparation time: 20 minutes, plus 30 minutes chilling
Cooking time: About 30 minutes

You can make these kebabs with lamb instead of beef if you like. They're beautifully flavoured and are perfect with the chutney.
Antony

WINNER

HEAVEN AND EARTH (HIMMEL UND ERDE)

BY FATHER RAINER

When its cold and chilly, this straightforward simple dish makes a warming meal. It's a natural choice for a light lunch or supper, but there isn't any reason why you can't enjoy it for breakfast as well. I'm a Benedictine monk at Ampleforth Abbey in Yorkshire, where I tend the Abbey's orchard – we grow 49 varieties of apple on 2000 trees. Before becoming a monk I trained as a doctor, and before that, I ran a small restaurant in Germany with a friend. This is a really straightforward peasant dish, traditional in the part of Germany I come from. I make simple food, in keeping with the monastic way of life, and I think that a sense of season and locality is very important – hence this recipe.

Ingredients

1 kg large potatoes, peeled
  and cut into chunks
1 kg strong-flavoured apples,
  such as Belle de Boskoop or Cockpit,
  peeled, cored and quartered
1–2 tbsp sugar, to taste
50 g butter
2 large onions, finely sliced
200 g smoked streaky bacon, diced
4 slices of black pudding
salt

1. Bring a large pan of salted water to the boil over a high heat. Add the potatoes and boil for 10–15 minutes until tender. While they are cooking, put the apples in another pan with a little water and the sugar, then simmer gently, stirring occasionally, until they are soft. When the potatoes are tender, drain off most of the water and mash roughly in the pan. Add the apples and their juices to the potatoes and stir until the apples start to disintegrate, but stop before they become a purée. Keep this mixture warm.

2. Melt half the butter in a frying pan over a medium heat. Add the onions and bacon and fry, stirring occasionally, for about 5 minutes, or until the onion is soft and the bacon has rendered its fat. Melt the remaining butter in another pan and fry the black pudding slices until they are cooked through and hot.

3. To serve, divide the potato and apple mixture, and onions and bacon, equally between four plates, making a pile of the potato mixture. Put a slice of black pudding on top of each one, and finish by pouring over some of the melted butter from the black pudding pan.

Servings: 4
Level of difficulty: Easy
Preparation time: 20 minutes
Cooking time: About 50 minutes

This is wonderful, you really get the separate tastes of the different ingredients. Lovely.
Paul

WINNER

GARLIC-BAKED CUSTARDS

BY KIRSTY SMALLWOOD

For a dinner party, these make an impressive first course – they are sophisticated with a lovely texture that isn't too heavy. I like to serve these with lightly fried mixed mushrooms on the side and accompanied with French bread. My mother was not a great cook but my ex-husband made a real effort to introduce me to good food and my interest just grew. I'm a big fan of organic food and have my own vegetable garden. I also love travelling, and usually go with a good friend who lives in San Francisco. About fifteen years ago she took me to a restaurant specially to eat this dish because it was so unusual – I thought it was wonderful. I like experimenting with the food I come across on my travels, so I decided to recreate it at home.

1. Preheat the oven to 180°C / gas 4. Grease six 125 ml ramekins or dariole moulds with the butter and put them to one side. Break up the garlic into cloves, leaving them unpeeled, then place all the cloves in a shallow ovenproof dish with the olive oil, water, thyme and bay leaves. Bake them in the oven for 45–60 minutes, until the garlic is really soft, then remove from the oven and set aside to cool.

2. Once the garlic cloves are cool, remove them from the cooking juices (reserve the juices). Gently squeeze the garlic flesh out of the papery skins into a bowl, then mash the flesh.

3. Combine the whole egg, the egg yolks, cream, cheese and 2 tablespoons of the garlicky cooking juices, including half the thyme leaves, in a bowl, then stir in the mashed garlic. Transfer the mixture to a food processor or blender and process it until really smooth. Season with a pinch of cayenne pepper and salt and pepper to taste.

4. Pour this custard mixture into the prepared ramekins, dividing it equally. Place the ramekins in a roasting tin containing enough hot water to come halfway up the sides of the dishes and bake for about 30 minutes, or until just set. Serve hot, turned out on to plates.

Ingredients

butter, for greasing
2 large heads elephant garlic, or 3 heads ordinary garlic, left whole
100 ml olive oil
200 ml water
2 tsp thyme leaves
2 bay leaves
1 egg
5 egg yolks
300 ml double cream
30 g Parmesan cheese, freshly grated
pinch of cayenne pepper
salt and pepper

This is probably one of the most 'cheffie' dishes we had in the programme, and it would be lovely for a dinner party.
Antony

Servings: 6
Level of difficulty: Intermediate
Preparation time: 25 minutes, plus cooling time
Cooking time: 1 hour 15 minutes to 1 hour 30 minutes

WINNER

STUFFED MEAT CAKE (KIBBI BI FURON)
BY EDITH KASHKOUSH

Everyone will take notice when you produce this Middle Eastern speciality – it makes a spectacular dish for a large gathering. I always serve it with a bowl of natural yogurt mixed with finely chopped mint and cucumber, and a green salad alongside. My husband, Marvi, is a Palestinian Catholic; I'm an Irish Protestant and we met when I was just a young girl – I'd gone to Kuwait with my family. Marvi's family left Palestine when the area they lived in became part of Israel – this traditional Middle-Eastern dish was taught to me by Marvi's mother and aunt. It holds happy memories of large family gatherings, and I really think that a family stays together by sharing food and sitting round a table. As proof that it works, we have been happily married for 31 years and have two sons!

1. Preheat the oven to 190°C / gas 5, and begin by making the stuffing mixture. Melt the butter in a large frying pan over a medium heat. Add the pine nuts and fry until golden. Then add the beef and continue cooking until the meat starts to brown. Add the onion and fry (stirring occasionally) until the meat is completely browned and the onions are transparent. Stir in the parsley, salt, pepper and allspice and cook for another couple of minutes before removing the pan from the heat and leaving the mixture to cool.

2. Now make the meat paste. Put the bulgur wheat in a large heat proof bowl and pour over enough boiling water to cover, then leave it for 10–15 minutes until the grains have softened. Process the beef in a food processor until it resembles a paste and then tip it into a large bowl. Drain the bulgur wheat and add to the beef along with the onion, salt, pepper and allspice. Mix everything well to form a smooth paste, adding a little cold water if it seems too dry. Divide the mix into two equal portions.

3. Grease a deep 30-cm springform cake tin with a little butter. Dip your hands in cold water and spread one half of the paste mixture so that it covers the base of the tin. Smooth it to an even level all over, dipping your hands in cold water again to prevent the paste sticking to you. Then spread the cooled stuffing mixture over the base layer.

4. Top with the second half of the mince paste, spreading it evenly. Then lightly score the top into 8–10 wedges, using a sharp knife. Garnish the cake by gently pushing in the extra pine nuts. Finally, pour the melted butter over the top, place the tin on a baking sheet and bake on the middle shelf of the oven for 35–40 minutes, until browned and firm to the touch.

5. Leave it to rest for a few minutes before cutting into wedges.

Ingredients
For the stuffing:
50 g butter, plus extra for the tin
80 g pine nuts
450 g minced beef
1 large onion, finely chopped
small bunch of flat-leaf parsley, finely chopped
1 tsp salt
¼ tsp freshly ground black pepper
¼ tsp ground allspice

For the meat paste:
350 g bulgur wheat
900 g lean minced beef
1 large onion, finely grated
2 tsp salt
½ tsp freshly ground black pepper
½ tsp ground allspice
1 tbsp pine nuts
70 g butter, melted

Servings: 8–10
Level of difficulty: Intermediate
Preparation time: 40 minutes
Cooking time: About 50 minutes

*Another exotic winner, a sort of Middle-Eastern
meatloaf with a lovely spiciness about it
which I really liked.
Paul*

WINNER

KOREAN BEEF (BULGOGI)
BY MARC MILLON

Try this recipe and add an Asian flavour to your next barbecue. 'Bulgogi' means 'fire meat' in Korean and the Koreans have a great tradition of cooking over charcoal, much like the British barbecue. This reminds me of my origins. I grew up in California but I was born in Mexico, though my mother was Korean and my father French, and I've been living in the UK for 30 years. This is a traditional recipe that my Korean grandmother used to cook, which has been passed down – my mother had her version and I've developed my own.

Ingredients

1.5 kg piece of lean rump steak,
    at least 2.5 cm thick
4 large garlic cloves, finely chopped
2.5 cm piece of fresh ginger, peeled
    and finely chopped
6 spring onions, shredded diagonally
100 ml soy sauce
4 tbsp vegetable oil
1 tbsp sesame oil
2 tbsp coarsely crushed black peppercorns
1 tbsp toasted sesame seeds

For the light vinaigrette:
100 ml groundnut oil
25 ml sherry vinegar
splash of soy sauce

For the salad and garnish:
mixed wild greens and herbs, such as wild
    rocket, dandelion leaves, fresh basil,
    flat-leaf parsley and coriander
6 spring onions, shredded diagonally
1 bunch of radishes, thinly sliced
large handful of fresh coriander,
    coarsely chopped
1 tbsp toasted sesame seeds,
    crushed with salt

1. Using a sharp knife, score the meat lightly in a diamond pattern and place in a large flat dish. Make a marinade by mixing together the garlic, ginger, spring onions, soy sauce, vegetable oil, sesame oil, black peppercorns and toasted sesame seeds. Pour this mixture over the meat, and rub it in with your hands. Leave the beef to marinate for about 1 hour, at room temperature.

2. Preheat the grill or heat a ridged cast-iron frying pan until it is very hot. Drain the meat, reserving the marinade, and pat it dry. Cook under the grill or in the hot pan for 2–3 minutes on each side; it should be charred on the outside but still rare inside. Transfer to a wooden board and leave it to rest for about 10 minutes. Meanwhile, tip the reserved marinade into a small pan, bring to the boil and boil hard for at least 2 minutes, then remove it from the heat.

3. Whisk all the vinaigrette ingredients together in a small bowl, then dress the leaves and herbs lightly with the vinaigrette and pile on to a large plate. Slice the beef and arrange over the dressed salad leaves. Pile the spring onions, radishes, coriander and sesame seeds on top of the meat, and spoon over a little of the marinade if liked. Serve straight away.

Servings: 6–8
Level of difficulty: Intermediate
Preparation time: 30 minutes, plus 1 hour marinating
Cooking time: 12 minutes

This looks gorgeous, and it's a wonderful recipe – I've not done anything like it before.
Antony

MEXICAN TACOS
BY MARIA PRICE

Ingredients

For the drunken beans:
500 g dried pinto or borlotti beans
2 tsp salt
2 big bunches of coriander,
  roughly chopped
oil, for shallow frying
6 rashers of smoked bacon, chopped
1 onion, finely chopped
1 beef tomato, chopped
2–3 green chillies, chopped
200 ml Mexican beer

For the cortadillo:
1 kg fillet steak, cut into 3 cm cubes
2 garlic cloves, crushed
½ tsp ground black pepper
3 tsp ground cumin
2 tsp salt
2 tbsp vegetable oil
1 onion, finely chopped
2 garlic cloves, finely chopped
2 potatoes, diced
1.25 kg tomatoes, peeled and chopped
2 green chillies, finely chopped, optional
3 tinned chipotle chillies, optional

For the tortillas:
500 g maize flour
700 ml warm water

For the guacamole:
2 ripe avocados
1 beef tomato, roughly chopped
4 spring onions, finely chopped
1 green chilli, finely chopped
bunch of coriander, chopped
juice of 1 lime
1 tsp rock salt

1. Make the drunken beans first. Cover the beans with 3 times the amount of cold water in a pressure cooker and cook for 1 hour 30 minutes, or until tender. Cool slightly, then uncover, add the salt, and boil them again for another 5 minutes. If you do not have a pressure cooker, soak the same quantity of dried beans overnight, then drain, rinse and put them in a large pan of unsalted water. Boil sharply for 10 minutes, then reduce the heat and simmer until the beans are tender, which could take 1–2 hours. However you cook them, once they are soft add half the coriander and take the pan off the heat. Don't drain the liquid from the beans.

2. Heat a little oil in a large frying pan over a medium heat. Add the bacon, onion, tomato and chillies and fry for 5–7 minutes, stirring often, until the onion is soft. Add the beans and boil, uncovered, for about 15 minutes, stirring now and then. Add the remaining coriander and the beer, stir well, turn off the heat and set aside.

3. For the cortadillo, put the steak in a bowl, add the crushed garlic, pepper, cumin and half the salt and mix well. Leave it in the fridge for 2 hours, though it can be left overnight. Heat the oil in a frying pan and fry the onion for 2–3 minutes, to soften. Add the chopped garlic and the marinated steak and cook, stirring, for 5 minutes. Add the diced potatoes and cook for 5 minutes more before adding the tomatoes, chillies and the remaining salt. Turn the heat down and simmer, uncovered, for about 10 minutes, or until the sauce has thickened and the meat and potatoes are tender.

4. Make the tortillas by mixing the flour and water in a bowl with your hands to make a dough, adding a little more water if necessary – you want it soft, not sticky. Cover the bowl and let the dough stand for 15 minutes. Then form it into small rounds the size of golf balls and use your hands to pat them out into round pancakes about 3 mm thick.

5. Heat a frying pan on a medium heat. Once it is hot, put a freshly made tortilla in the pan and, when the edges start lifting, turn it over and cook for a minute. Turn it a second time and it should puff up. Repeat this with the other tortillas, keeping them warm until you are ready to serve everything.

6. Now prepare the guacamole. Cut the avocado in half, take out the stone (save it) and scoop the flesh into a bowl. Roughly mash it with a fork, then add the chopped tomato, spring onions, chilli, coriander, lime juice and a little salt and mix well. Put the stone in the middle of the bowl to keep the avocado from discolouring.

7. To serve, put a warm tortilla on a plate and fill with the cortadillo, warmed drunken beans or the guacamole, or use a mixture of all three in one tortilla. Roll to make a wrap and eat them with your hands!

Servings: 6
Level of difficulty: Intermediate
Preparation time: 40 minutes plus marinating
Cooking time: 2 hours 30 minutes

Terrific. Having lived in California, I miss the taste of real Mexican food – and this has that authenticity.
Paul

WINNER

CHICKEN EARLE
BY ANN KEELING

I'm a single mum with four sons, so need quick, delicious recipes that can fill up growing boys. This family favourite, which never fails to please, came from my home economics teacher, Mrs Earle, 30 years ago – though she doesn't know that our entire family call it after her! I cooked from an early age and loved it, and my boys all love it as well. I work full time but still make time to cook as I think that making good food for my sons is one of the best ways there is of showing that I love them. I learned many recipes from my mother and have passed those on to the boys, too.

1. Preheat the oven to 190°C / gas 5. Heat the butter and oil in a large, heavy-bottomed frying pan over a medium heat. Add the chicken pieces and fry, stirring, for about 5 minutes, or until browned. Add the bacon and garlic to the pan and continue cooking for a few minutes, stirring, until the bacon gives off its fat and becomes crisp. Tip in the celery and leek, and stir for a further few minutes until the vegetables soften.

2. Reduce the heat to medium-low. Sprinkle in the flour and cook, stirring around for 2 minutes to cook out the raw taste. Gradually stir in the milk and chicken stock to make a smooth sauce. Add the mushrooms and parsley. Transfer the contents of the pan to a large baking dish and smooth the surface.

3. Make the topping by mixing the breadcrumbs and grated cheese together. Sprinkle this generously over the top. Put the dish on a baking sheet and bake for 15–20 minutes until the topping is crisp. Serve piping hot.

Ingredients
25 g butter
1 tbsp olive oil
5 boneless, skinless chicken breasts, chopped
5 bacon rashers, rinds removed if necessary, chopped
2 large or 3 medium garlic cloves, finely chopped
2 celery sticks, chopped
1 leek, sliced and rinsed
25 g plain flour
150 ml milk
150 ml chicken stock
25 g button mushrooms, wiped and quartered
bunch of fresh flat-leaf parsley, chopped
salt and pepper

For the topping:
55 g fresh breadcrumbs
55 g cheese, such as Cheddar, grated

Servings: 5
Level of difficulty: Easy
Preparation time: 15 minutes
Cooking time: 30 minutes

Here's a great family dish which looks terrific – just the sort of thing that kids will devour. It could easily become a staple.
Paul

WINNER

ETHIOPIAN CHICKEN
(DORO WATT)
BY SEFANIT SIRAK-KEBEDE

I am Ethiopian, and this traditional recipe reminds me of happy times before the revolution, when I cooked at home with my mother. It's been passed down through generations, and I often cook it at the Ethiopian Community Centre for celebrations. In the past, every young girl had to prove her culinary knowledge to her husband, by making Doro Watt. Ideally, serve this chicken dish with homemade cottage cheese and Enjera, Ethiopian teff-grain bread, which can be bought from African shops.

1. Prepare the clarified butter by melting the butter in a frying pan over a very low heat. Stir in the red onion, coriander, ginger and garlic and simmer for 40 minutes. Using a sieve lined with a piece of muslin (or a sterilised J-cloth), strain the mixture into a bowl. Reserve the strained and clarified butter and discard any residue left in the sieve.

2. Now make the sauce for the chicken. Put the onions in a large pan over a very low heat with about 1 large ladleful of clarified butter. Cook them gently, stirring occasionally and adding a dash of water to prevent the onions from sticking and burning, until they take on a deep brown colour. This can take up to an hour. It's best to cook them with the lid on until they're really soft, then take off the lid and continue cooking until browned.

3. Once the onions are ready, stir in the berbere and the garlic and ginger mixture. Cook gently for up to a further hour, stirring occasionally, until you have a creamy paste, adding drizzles of water along the way to prevent sticking. Stir in another 2 ladlefuls of clarified butter and simmer for about 30 minutes, stirring occasionally.

4. While the sauce is simmering, cut the chicken into 12 pieces (discard the parson's nose for authenticity – Ethiopians consider it unclean). Wash the chicken pieces, then put them in a large bowl of fresh water to which you have added the lemon juice. Leave them to soak for 30 minutes, then drain well.

5. Add the chicken pieces to the sauce in the pan, with the coriander, water and salt to taste. Stir thoroughly to mix, then bring gently to the boil. Reduce the heat and simmer for 30–40 minutes, or until the chicken is cooked through. Meanwhile, bring a separate pan of water to the boil, reduce the heat and lower the eggs into the simmering water. Cook the eggs for 10–15 minutes until very hard boiled. Drain and cover with cold water to cool them slightly.

6. Peel the eggs and score around each one several times using a sharp knife, so that when the eggs are added to the chicken mixture they will soak up some of the sauce but remain whole. Add the eggs to the cooked chicken mixture and stir gently to coat the eggs with the sauce.

Ingredients

For the clarified butter:

500 g butter
1 small red onion, finely chopped
2 tsp ground coriander
2 tsp finely chopped garlic
2 tsp finely chopped ginger

For the chicken:

1 kg red onions, finely chopped
2–3 ladlefuls clarified butter (see above)
1½ tbsp berbere
   (Ethiopian chilli powder), available from
   African shops
1 tbsp mixed crushed garlic and finely
   chopped peeled fresh ginger
1 large boiling fowl or chicken
juice of 2 lemons
1 tbsp ground coriander
1–2 ladlefuls water
salt
12 eggs

Servings: 4–5
Level of difficulty: Intermediate
Preparation time: 40 minutes
Cooking time: 4 hours

It's great to see something as authentic as this; it could well become part of my own repertoire.
Paul

LEFTOVER CHRISTMAS TURKEY PIE

BY JUDY GOODMAN

Comfort cooking doesn't get better than this – give festive turkey a makeover in this golden-topped pastry pie, crammed with succulent meat and vegetables.

1. Make the giblet gravy the night before you make the pie, though you can use good stock or even an appropriate soup instead if you wish. For the gravy, place all the ingredients in a large saucepan over a medium heat, partially cover the pan and leave to simmer for at least 3 hours, skimming the surface as necessary. Keep an eye on the water level and top up as necessary. Strain, discarding the giblets, vegetables and bouquet garni, and leave the liquid to cool. Cover and put in the fridge overnight – once it is cold you can remove all the fat from the top. The next day bring the gravy to the boil and thicken it with the flour, cornflour or brown gravy powder mixed to a paste with a little water.

2. Grease a 24 cm ovenproof flan dish. Make the pastry by first mixing the eggs and water together and putting them in the fridge. Then put the plain flour in a bowl and chill that in the fridge for 15–20 minutes; the cooler it is, the better the pastry. Empty the chilled flour into a food processor. Add the butter and blitz until combined and the mixture resembles crumbs. Add the egg and water mixture and process again to form a dough. Remove this from the processor and knead lightly until smooth. Roll out two-thirds of the dough to the size of the flan dish on a lightly floured surface, and carefully line the dish. Roll out the remaining dough for the top of the pie and put both in the fridge until you are ready to use them.

3. Preheat the oven to 200°C / gas 6, and make the filling. Heat the goose fat in a heavy-based pan over a medium heat. Add the onions and fry, stirring occasionally, for about 5 minutes until softened. Add the mushrooms and continue frying until they give off their liquid, then leave the mixture to cool. Add the turkey, carrots and giblet gravy to the cooled onion mixture and stir everything together. Put this mixture into the lined flan dish and dampen the edges of the pastry base with water. Cover the dish with the reserved pastry from the fridge and crimp the edges together. Use any trimmings of dough to decorate the top, and make a small hole in the centre to allow steam to escape. Brush with beaten egg and place the pie on a baking sheet. Bake for about 30 minutes, or until the pastry is golden and the filling is piping hot.

Ingredients

For the giblet gravy:
giblets from the turkey
2–2.5 litres water
1 carrot, chopped
1 leek, trimmed, chopped and rinsed
1 bouquet garni
1 tbsp plain flour, cornflour or brown
   gravy powder

For the pastry:
4 small eggs, beaten
2 tbsp iced water
500 g plain flour, plus extra for dusting
250g butter, diced, plus extra for the dish
little beaten egg, to glaze

For the pie filling:
2 tbsp goose fat
1 small onion, chopped
6 medium mushrooms, chopped
250 g skinless cooked turkey, chopped
3 carrots, sliced and lightly cooked
225 ml giblet gravy

Beautiful pastry and lovely juices to this pie. You can add other leftover vegetables, too.
Antony

Servings: 6
Level of difficulty: Intermediate
Preparation time: 3 hours 20 minutes, plus
20 minutes chilling for dough
Cooking time: 35 minutes

POTATO SCONES
BY HUGH SMITH

These are a tempting teatime treat, especially when served hot with plenty of melting butter.

1. Bring a large pan of salted water to the boil over a high heat. Add the potatoes and boil for 15–20 minutes, or until tender. Drain them well, then mash. Add the flour, olive oil, salt and pepper to the mashed potatoes and bind everything together thoroughly. The amount of flour you need will vary depending on the moistness of the potatoes, but make sure there is no stickiness to the mixture once everything is combined.

2. Roll out half the dough on a lightly floured surface to a circle about 5 mm thick, then prick all over the surface with a fork. Heat a little olive oil in a heavy-based frying pan over a medium heat. Carefully place the whole potato scone round in the pan, then cut it into quarters using a blunt knife. Cook the scones until they are golden brown underneath, then flip them over and cook the other sides until they are also golden brown.

3. Put the scones on a warmed plate and serve piping hot with lashings of butter. Repeat with the other half of the dough to make a total of eight potato scones.

Ingredients

1 kg floury potatoes, such as
    King Edwards, peeled and chopped
250 g plain flour, plus extra for dusting
4 tbsp olive oil, plus extra for frying
salt and pepper
butter, to serve

A definite winner for me. I grew up with potato scones, and these would be fantastic with bacon and eggs...
Paul

Servings: 8
Level of difficulty: Easy
Preparation time: 20 minutes
Cooking time: 35–40 minutes

CHICKEN WITH PUY LENTILS COOKED IN CIDER
BY BEN TICEHURST

Try this comforting one-dish meal when you want to make sure you are eating healthily. It's packed with protein for energy and lots of flavour. The small, green-grey Puy lentils are ideal to use because they hold their shape. I became interested in cooking simply because I'm greedy! I've travelled widely with my wife and picked up recipes along the way, but this one is actually from her grandmother. She's a foodie, too, and I think our common interest has really helped our relationship. I adapted this so I could use the cider my uncle makes – it's wine in the original recipe. I've just taken up surfing with my mates and I'm the first one to get into a surfing magazine – in the background of a photograph, though, and I'm cooking rather than surfing!

1. Heat 1 tablespoon of the oil in a heavy-based pan over a low heat. Add the bacon and fry for 1 minute, then stir in the onion and garlic and fry for about 5 minutes, or until the onion has softened.

2. Pick over the lentils to ensure there are no small stones included and rinse them well. Add them to the pan and stir well, coating them with oil. Pour in the cider, add the bay leaf and thyme, and bring to the boil. Cover the pan, reduce the heat and simmer gently for 25–30 minutes. Stir the lentils occasionally as they cook, adding a dash of water if they look like sticking, until they have softened but still hold their shape. Preheat the oven to 180°C/gas 4.

3. Meanwhile, season the chicken breasts with salt and pepper. Heat the remaining oil in an ovenproof pan over a medium-high heat and fry the seasoned chicken pieces on both sides until golden. Leave them in the pan, skin side up, and roast in the oven for 10 minutes, or until cooked through. When the chicken is ready, drain the lentils of any remaining liquid (they will have absorbed most of it) and serve the chicken on top of them. Sprinkle with the chopped parsley before bringing to the table.

Ingredients
3 tbsp olive oil
3 rashers of unsmoked streaky bacon, rinds removed if necessary and cut into strips
1 onion, chopped
1 garlic clove, finely chopped
200g Puy lentils
1 litre cider
1 bay leaf
sprig of thyme
4 x 175g chicken breasts
2 tbsp finely chopped flat-leaf parsley
salt and pepper

Good, hearty stuff – and with low GI cooking all the rage, this deserves its place in **The People's Cookbook.**
Antony

Servings: 4
Level of difficulty: Easy
Preparation time: 10 minutes
Cooking time: About 40 minutes

WINNER

TOURNEDOS ROSSINI WITH CHEESE AND ONION POTATO AND RATATOUILLE

BY ANDY TYNEMOUTH

Big on bold mediterranean flavours, this meaty steak and garlicky ratatouille is my ultimate party piece for impressing friends. Even though I'm a fitness fanatic, I find it hard to resist the attraction of its saucy, boozy accompaniment.

1. Preheat the oven to 180°C / gas 4. Put the potatoes in a pan of salted cold water and bring to the boil over a high heat. Reduce the heat and leave them to simmer for 5 minutes, then drain and set aside to cool.

2. Lightly grease a shallow ovenproof dish with a little of the butter. Cut the cooled potatoes into slices about 5 mm thick and place a layer of these slices in the dish. Then sprinkle half of the two cheeses, half the herbs and half the onion over them. Season with salt and pepper and dot with the remaining butter. Place another layer of potatoes on top, and repeat. The last layer of potatoes does not need to cover the whole of the top of the dish. Pour the beaten egg over the potatoes and put them in the oven for about 20 minutes, or until golden brown.

3. Now prepare the ratatouille. Heat the olive oil in a frying pan over a medium heat. Add the onion and garlic and fry gently for 4–5 minutes. Stir in the courgette and and continue cooking for another 4–5 minutes, then add the tomatoes and herbs. Cover the pan and leave the vegetables to gently cook for about 15 minutes, or until they are all tender.

4. Meanwhile, prepare the tournedos. Heat the olive oil in a frying pan over a medium-high heat. Add the bread and fry on both sides until golden to make croutons; keep them warm. Season the steaks with salt and pepper, then fry them in a very hot pan for 2–3 minutes on each side (for rare-cooked beef). Tip the brandy into the pan and set it alight and let it flame until the brandy has burned off.

5. Now remove the steaks from the pan, cover and keep them warm. Pour most of the wine into the pan over a high heat and scrape the base with a wooden spoon to 'deglaze', then add the stock and bring to the boil, and continue boiling until the sauce reduces a little. Mix the cornflour with the remaining red wine, then add it to the sauce and stir well to combine everything. Continue boiling for a minute to thicken the sauce, then season it to taste and keep warm.

6. Spread a good dollop of pâté on each of the croutons and place them on warm serving plates. Top with the steaks, pour over the sauce and serve with potatoes and ratatouille.

Ingredients

For the potatoes:
4 large potatoes, preferably Vivaldi, cut in half
25 g butter
125 g mature Cheddar, grated
125 g Wensleydale cheese, grated
1 tbsp chopped flat leaf parsley
1 tbsp snipped chives
1 small red onion, finely chopped
1 small egg, lightly beaten
salt and pepper

For the ratatouille:
1 tbsp olive oil
1 small onion, chopped
1 garlic clove, finely chopped
1 courgette, cut into chunks
4 plum tomatoes, chopped
1 tbsp chopped flat-leaf parsley

For the tournedos:
2 tbsp olive oil
4 slices of French stick, about 1.5 cm thick
4 fillet steaks, about 150 g each, from the thinner end of the fillet
100 ml Armagnac brandy
250 ml good red wine, Barolo ideally
250 ml chicken stock
1 tbsp cornflour
100 g coarse chicken liver pâté
salt and pepper

Servings: 4
Level of difficulty: Intermediate
Preparation time: 20 minutes
Cooking time: 45 minutes

This is an old classic that Andy has adapted;
it would be an excellent dish for a dinner party.
Antony

WINNER

AFRICAN PILAFF
BY SAMARA ROLT

My mother is from Zanzibar and my father is British, and I'm really proud of my background – Zanzibar is on the 'spice route' and it's a real mix of African and Indian culture. This particular dish is my favourite; it was something we had for special occasions and family celebrations when I was growing up. In fact, we still have it now whenever I go home, and my mother taught it to me. Being of mixed race you can sometimes feel isolated, and food – this dish especially – is really important; it's a way of sharing and celebrating your heritage.

Ingredients

For the chicken and potatoes:
6 skinless chicken thighs
(preferably free range)
juice of ½ lemon
4 garlic cloves, finely chopped
2.5 cm piece fresh ginger, peeled
and grated
2 waxy potatoes, quartered
850 ml–1.2 litres chicken stock
salt and pepper

For the rice:
200 g basmati rice
3 tbsp vegetable oil
2 onions, finely chopped
2 garlic cloves, finely chopped
1 tbsp cumin seeds
½ tsp ground cardamom (or seeds from 6
whole pods, crushed)
½ tsp ground cinnamon
1 tsp ground cumin
1 tsp sea salt
55 g raisins

For the chilli salad:
1 large onion, thinly sliced
1 tbsp granulated sugar
2 bird's-eye chillies, deseeded
and finely chopped
7.5 cm piece cucumber,
cut into 1 cm pieces
2 vine-ripened tomatoes,
cut into 1 cm pieces
small bunch of coriander, chopped

1. Begin by preparing the chicken. Season the chicken thighs by rubbing them all over with the lemon juice, garlic and ginger. Sprinkle them with a pinch or two of salt and pepper and put them in a shallow, non-metallic dish. Cover it and leave them in the fridge for at least 2 hours, or preferably overnight.

2. Put the marinated chicken in a large saucepan with the potatoes, and add enough stock to cover the chicken and potatoes completely. Bring to the boil, then reduce the heat, cover the pan and simmer for about 30 minutes, or until the chicken is cooked and tender. Transfer the chicken and potatoes to a plate using a slotted spoon, cover and keep them warm in a low oven. Reserve 425 ml of the stock for cooking the rice.

3. Rinse the rice in cold water, then cover it with fresh water and leave it to soak for 10 minutes. Drain it well and put it to one side.

4. Heat the vegetable oil in a large saucepan over a medium to high heat. Add the onions, cover, and fry for about 10 minutes, or until they are golden brown, stirring occasionally. Add the garlic, all the spices and the salt and fry for a further 5 minutes, or until the aroma of the spices comes through. Add the rice and fry over a medium heat for 3 minutes, or until the rice is coated. Add the reserved chicken stock and bring the stock to the boil, then reduce the heat to the lowest possible level. Cover the pan with foil and the lid (so no steam escapes) and simmer for about 20 minutes or until the rice is tender. Stir in the raisins 5 minutes before the end of the cooking time.

5. Make the chilli salad while the rice is cooking. Put the onion in a heatproof bowl, sprinkle it with the sugar and then cover with boiling water, stirring to dissolve the sugar. Set it aside for 10 minutes. Drain the onions and place them in a serving bowl, then add the chillies, cucumber, tomatoes and coriander (reserving 1 tablespoon of coriander for the garnish) and toss everything well to mix the ingredients together. Set the salad aside.

6. Now return to the chicken. Remove the meat from the bones and discard the bones. When the rice is cooked, gently stir in the chicken and potatoes, mixing well. Spoon the chicken and rice mixture onto a warm serving platter and sprinkle it with the remaining coriander. Garnish the pilaff with toasted flaked almonds and serve with plain yoghurt.

A well-deserved win; a good family dish with loads of flavour.
Antony

Servings: 4
Level of difficulty: Intermediate
Preparation time: 25 minutes,
plus overnight marinating
Cooking time: 1 hour

WINNER

VEGGIE COTTAGE PIE
BY KARDIEN GERBRANDS

Ingredients

2 tbsp extra virgin olive oil
225 g textured vegetable protein (TVP)
2 large onions, thinly sliced
1 large leek, thinly sliced and rinsed
2 medium carrots, diced
3 celery sticks, finely chopped
large handful of purple sprouting
  broccoli, including leaves, chopped
6 red-skinned potatoes, peeled
  and cut into chunks
100 ml milk
50 g butter
75 g mature Cheddar cheese, grated
salt and pepper

I do nearly all the cooking at home and I'm sure there are many cooks who appreciate the problem I have to deal with on a daily basis – I'm a vegetarian and the rest of the family eats meat. This flavoursome dish is one of my favourites as it is filling and comforting enough that no one misses the meat for one meal, but it can easily be adapted to keep carnivores happy. I run numerous farmers' markets in Gloucestershire, and fresh, seasonal ingredients are important to me. In fact, it was seeing all the lovely local meat on offer at the markets that persuaded my wife to eat meat again. People are sometimes surprised to see me in the kitchen, but my father also did a lot of cooking when I was growing up, especially the Sunday roast, so I've always thought it was quite normal for men to cook.

1. Heat the olive oil in a large frying pan over a medium heat. Add the textured vegetable protein and onions and fry, stirring, for about 5 minutes, or until the onions are soft. Add the leek, carrots, celery and broccoli and cover the pan, reduce the heat to low and leave to simmer for 20 minutes, stirring occasionally, or until the vegetables are tender. Towards the end of the cooking time, preheat the oven to 200°C / gas 6 and grease a large ovenproof dish.

2. While the vegetables are cooking, make the mash for the topping. Bring a pan of salted water to the boil. Add the potatoes and boil for 15 minutes, or until very tender. Drain the potatoes well, then put them in a bowl and mash, gradually adding the milk, followed by the butter. Stir in a good handful of the cheese, then taste and adjust the seasoning if necessary.

3. Tip the cooked vegetables into the dish and smooth the surface. Spoon the mashed potatoes on top and sprinkle with the remaining cheese. Place the dish on a baking sheet and bake for 10–15 minutes until the filling is hot and the cheese is melted and golden.

Servings: 4
Level of difficulty: Intermediate
Preparation time: 20 minutes
Cooking time: About 45 minutes

A cottage pie is great comfort food. This one smells wonderful and the flavours come together nicely – if you're not vegetarian you could easily use meat.
Paul

WINNER

SPICED GUJARATI POTATO BALLS (BATETA WADA)
BY BILL MESWANIA

These fragrant, golden potato balls with a creamy yogurt dip make an ideal snack for when vegetarian friends are visiting – non-veggies will find them hard to resist as well!

My family came to the UK in the 1970s as Ugandan refugees. We were in a camp on Dartmoor at first and the food was a shock – after a week the women approached the organisers and asked to be allowed into the kitchen. Our family had originally come from Gujarat in western India which is a very religious state; the cooking is traditionally vegetarian, based on the principle of Ahimsa, non-violence to all creatures. I became completely vegetarian myself when I was 21. This is a traditional snack I would serve to guests visiting my home.

1. Bring a large saucepan of salted water to the boil. Add the potatoes and boil for 15–20 minutes until they are tender. Drain them well. When they are cool enough to handle, peel them and mash with the garlic purée, ginger, chilli paste, coriander, ground cumin and turmeric, garam masala, sugar and salt. Stir in the lemon juice and mix everything together. Roll the mixture into about golf ball-sized shapes and set them aside.

2. Now make the batter by mixing the gram flour with the salt and bicarbonate of soda then stir in enough water to make a thick batter. Heat enough oil for deep-frying in a deep-fat fryer or heavy-based saucepan until it reaches 180°–190°C, or when a cube of bread browns in 60 seconds. Dip the potato balls into the gram flour batter, shaking off the excess. Add the potato balls in batches and fry for 2 minutes, or until they are golden and crisp. Remove with a slotted spoon and transfer to a plate lined with kitchen paper to drain. Keep them warm in a low oven while you fry the remaining potato balls. It is important not to overcrowd the pan and return the oil to the correct temperature between batches, so the potato balls do not become soggy.

3. To make the dip, mix the yoghurt, mint vinegar (or fresh mint) and garlic salt together, adding a little salt. Serve with the crunchy potato balls.

Ingredients
8 potatoes, unpeeled and cut into chunks
1 tsp garlic purée
1 tsp grated fresh ginger
½–1 tsp green chilli paste, to taste
handful of chopped fresh coriander
1 tsp ground cumin
¼ tsp ground turmeric
½ tsp garam masala
1½ tsp sugar
2 tsp salt, plus extra for boiling
    the potatoes
3 tsp lemon juice

For the batter:
230 g fine gram flour (chickpea flour)
1 tsp salt
½ tsp bicarbonate of soda
vegetable oil for deep frying

For the dip:
100 ml plain yoghurt
1 tsp mint vinegar or chopped fresh mint
pinch of garlic salt

> *This is genuinely delicious, and something I've not come across before. The combination with the mint dip is lovely.*
> *Paul*

Servings: Makes about 18 balls
Level of difficulty: Intermediate
Preparation time: 20 minutes
Cooking time: About 30 minutes

ANTONY'S CHOICE

ANTIPASTI
BY ANGELA DE LUCA

Ingredients

Bruschetta:
250 g cherry tomatoes, diced
1 garlic clove, finely chopped
2 tbsp olive oil
salt and pepper
6 basil leaves
1 ciabatta loaf, cut into thin slices

Tuscan bean dip:
4 tbsp extra virgin olive oil
2 large onions, thinly sliced
pinch of sugar
2 x 420 g tins cannellini beans,
    rinsed and drained
60 ml chicken stock
1 tbsp chopped flat leaf parsley
salt and pepper

Spicy aubergine dip:
2 large aubergines, cut into 2 cm cubes
3 large red peppers
1 large onion, cut into 2 cm cubes
1 tsp sea salt
1 tsp ground black pepper
1 tbsp dried chilli flakes
3 large garlic cloves, finely chopped
135 ml extra virgin olive oil
2 tbsp chopped flat leaf parsley

Marinated red peppers and courgettes:
2 red peppers
2 courgettes, sliced lengthwise
150 ml light olive oil
2 tbsp red wine vinegar
2 garlic cloves, thinly sliced
2 tbsp chopped flat leaf parsley
pinch of salt

To serve:
fresh Parmesan, thinly sliced Parma ham,
    Italian salami, baguettes

1. Begin well before you want to serve the Antipasti – even the day before. For the tomato topping for the bruschetta place the tomatoes in a bowl and add the garlic and olive oil and season with salt and pepper. Put the basil leaves in a pile, roll them together tightly and slice through the roll of leaves to create strips. Stir these through the tomatoes, cover the bowl and leave the tomatoes for up to a day in the fridge.

2. For the bean dip, place 1 tablespoon of the olive oil in a frying pan over a medium heat. Add the onion and stir in the salt and the sugar. Reduce the heat, cover the pan and cook, stirring occasionally, for 10–15 minutes, until the onions are caramelised.

3. Put three-quarters of the beans in a blender or food processor. Add the stock, the remaining olive oil, a little salt and pepper. Add half the onions and process until you have a coarse paste. Empty this into a serving dish and mix in the remaining beans. Garnish the dip with the remaining onions, a sprinkle of parsley and a drizzle of olive oil. Cover it and put it in the fridge.

4. For the aubergine dip, preheat the oven to 200°C / gas 6. Place the aubergines, peppers and onions in a large bowl and add the salt, pepper, chilli flakes, garlic and olive oil. Stir well to coat the vegetable cubes and spread them evenly on 2 baking sheets. Put these in the oven and roast for 20–30 minutes until the vegetables are soft and golden. Allow them to cool, then pulse in a blender or food processor until they form a smooth paste. Stir the parsley through the dip, spoon it into a serving bowl, and cover and place in the fridge.

5. Now make the marinated peppers and courgettes. Hold the peppers over a gas ring with tongs until they are shrivelled and blackened (if you don't have a gas ring you can blacken them under a grill). Place them in a bowl, cover with cling film and leave to cool.

6. Heat a ridged cast-iron pan over a very high heat until it is smoking hot. Add the courgette slices and cook for 1 minute on each side or until charred lines appear. Place them in a deep dish. Peel off the charred skin, remove any seeds and cut the pepper flesh into thin strips, then scatter them over the courgette slices. Whisk the olive oil, vinegar, garlic and parsley together, along with a good pinch of salt and pour this over the peppers and courgettes. Leave them to marinate for 15 minutes.

7. Prepare everything for serving. Remove the dips from the fridge, and arrange the cheese, Parma ham and salami on a large platter with the baguettes. Just before you are ready to serve, finish the bruschetta; toast the ciabatta slices until they are golden and place a spoonful of tomatoes, along with their juices, on top of each one. Serve straight away.

Servings: 6–8
Level of difficulty: Intermediate
Preparation time: 1 hour, plus up to a day
marinating
Cooking time: About 1 hour 10 minutes

*I was shocked when this didn't win, as it
has such a great balance of different tastes.*
Antony

MAINS

WINNER

FENNEL-STUFFED SEA BASS PARCELS

BY STAN WAITE

I was brought up in Liverpool but now live in Whitby. I'm a fishmonger and also a mad keen fisherman; I've even converted my wife and we go fishing together. I often cook this dish for my wife – it was the first thing I made for her when we were courting, she loves it, and I always make it for her if she's had a bad week. Bass is my favourite fish, but I've only managed to catch a single one in thirty years of trying!

Ingredients

4 fennel bulbs
4 whole sea bass, approx 400 g each,
    gutted, scaled and rinsed inside and out
    with head and tail left on
2 tbsp olive oil
2 lemons, finely sliced
juice of 4 limes
large bunch of fresh coriander,
    finely chopped
salt and pepper

1. Preheat the oven to 200°C / gas 6. Remove the stalks and the tough outer layers of the fennel and coarsely grate the bulbs. Fill the cavity of each fish with the grated fennel and season with salt and pepper.

2. Cut 4 large pieces of foil and fold each one in half, so that you have a double piece of foil large enough to wrap around the fish. Brush the foil with a little olive oil and place a stuffed sea bass on top of each rectangle. Top the fish with lemon slices, pour the juice of a lime over each one, and finally add a sprinkling of fresh coriander. Seal the parcels tightly by folding the foil up around the fish and scrunching the tops together – be careful not to pierce the foil and make sure they are well sealed so none of the juices escape while the fish are cooking.

3. Place the parcels on a baking sheet, and bake for 25 minutes. To check the fish is cooked, open one of the parcels and insert a knife along the backbone. The flesh should flake easily and the juices will be milky white. Open the parcels at the table, as doing so releases a delicious aroma.

Fennel and seafood is a beautiful combination and this lovely dish is no exception.
Paul

Servings: 4
Level of difficulty: Easy
Preparation time: 15 minutes
Cooking time: 25 minutes

WINNER

STUFFED SPICED SALMON
BY NOOR JEHAN DEHANI

I was raised in Pakistan, and my mother taught me to cook. I was made to help in the kitchen when I was eleven, and I cried because my brother didn't have to help too, even threatening to run away! Now I love cooking, especially if I'm entertaining, for a family gathering or special occasion. I've been cooking in a tiny galley kitchen and it's like playing chess with pots and pans. I like to throw in my own ideas and even cut corners – my mother would not approve – this dish is inspired by Indian flavours.

Ingredients

For the herb paste:
5 green chillies (thin Indian or Kenyan variety), finely chopped
3 garlic cloves, finely chopped
5 sprigs of fresh coriander, finely chopped
2 tsp grated fresh ginger
1 large bunch of basil
1 large bunch of coriander
1 large bunch of dill
100 ml lemon juice
2 tbsp olive oil
salt

For the fish:
1.8 kg salmon, gutted and rinsed inside and out with head and tail left on
2 lemons, thinly sliced, to garnish
250 g cooked king prawns, to garnish

1. Preheat the oven to 190°C / gas 5, and prepare the herb paste. Combine the chillies, two thirds of the garlic and coriander in a pestle and mortar and work it into a paste, then add the remaining garlic and ginger and mix in well. Roughly chop two-thirds of the basil, half the coriander and half the dill. Add these to the paste with the lemon juice, then stir in the olive oil and a pinch of salt.

2. Lightly grease a piece of foil large enough to wrap completely around the salmon. Put the fish on to the foil, then stuff it with about a third of the herb paste. Smear the rest over the outside of the fish, reserving 1 tablespoon for the prawns. Sprinkle the remaining dill sprigs and herb leaves over the salmon and then gather up the foil to make a parcel. The foil should be airtight, but should also leave some space around the fish to allow the heat to circulate. Put the parcel on a baking sheet and bake the fish for 45 minutes, or until the flesh flakes easily and the juices are milky white when you insert a knife along the backbone.

3. Remove the fish from the oven and the foil. Place it on a serving platter and remove the skin (but leave the head and tail). Pour over any juices and arrange the lemon slices across the fish in an overlapping pattern.

4. Just before the fish finishes cooking, heat the remaining herb paste in a pan over a medium heat. When it is warm, remove the pan from the heat and add the cooked king prawns. Garnish the salmon with the herbed prawns and serve straight away.

It's nice to have a spicy salmon dish that actually works.
Paul

Servings: 6–8
Level of difficulty: Intermediate
Preparation time: 30 minutes
Cooking time: 45 minutes

LUXURY FISH PIE
BY JOE COOKE

1. Preheat the oven to 220°C / gas 7, and grease a large ovenproof serving dish. To make the mashed potato topping, bring a large pan of salted water to the boil over a high heat. Add the potatoes and boil for 15–20 minutes until tender. Drain well and mash with the butter until smooth, then set aside.

2. To make the filling, melt half the butter with half the oil in a large saucepan over a medium heat. Add the onions, half the garlic and all the mushrooms and fry, stirring occasionally, for about 5 minutes, or until the onions are softened. Add salt and pepper to taste, then remove the pan from the heat and set aside.

3. Melt the remaining butter and oil in a large frying pan over a medium heat. Add the remaining garlic and salt and pepper and stir around. Add the lobster flesh and quickly toss it in the hot oil, then remove it from the pan and set aside. Tip the scallops into the fat remaining in the pan, season them with salt and pepper and toss for 2–3 minutes, then remove and set aside. Add the salmon to the pan and cook for 3–4 minutes. Remove it, reserving any fish juices, and separate the fish into large flakes. Gently combine all the filling ingredients in a large bowl.

4. Make the cheese sauce by melting the butter in a pan over a low heat and stirring in the flour to make a roux, then cook, stirring for a few minutes. Put any reserved fish juices into a measuring jug and make up to 850 ml with milk. Gradually whisk this liquid into the roux and bring it to the boil. Reduce the heat and cook the sauce until thickened, stirring constantly. Check the seasoning and then add the cheese, followed by the wine. The sauce should now have the consistency of thin custard. Add it to the fish mixture in the large bowl and mix everything together. Spoon it into the ovenproof dish.

5. Spoon or pipe the mashed potato on top of the filling. Place the dish on a baking sheet and cook the pie for 30 minutes, until golden brown and bubbling.

Ingredients
For the mashed potato topping:
5 large floury potatoes, peeled
50 g butter
salt

For the filling:
30 g butter
2 tbsp vegetable oil
3 onions, finely chopped
8 garlic cloves, finely chopped
450 g button mushrooms,
    wiped and finely chopped
2 x 675–900 g lobsters, cooked,
    shelled and diced
1 kg scallops, shelled, trimmed and diced
1 side of salmon, skinned, deboned
    and chopped
salt and pepper

For the cheese sauce:
75 g butter
3 tbsp plain white flour
500 ml milk, approximate quantity
450 g mature Cheddar cheese,
    freshly grated
150 ml dry white wine

A fantastic dish. Fish pie is wonderful any time, but with all these fabulous ingredients it's great for a special occasion.
Antony

Servings: 6–8
Level of difficulty: Intermediate
Preparation time: 25 minutes
Cooking time: 1 hour 20 minutes

WINNER

FRIED FISH WITH ONION SALSA
(PESCADO FRITO CON SALSA DE CEBOLLA)
BY ROCIO O'LEARY

I am from Ecuador, where I met my Welsh husband while he was travelling. We fell in love and I came to Wales five years ago. The aromas of South American food remind me of home and without them I would die of homesickness. All my recipes come from my mother and I used to eat this dish at the seaside when I was a child; it's a traditional Ecuadorean recipe. In Ecuador people get together to eat and talk, and I remember how my mother, grandmother and aunts would gather in the kitchen to cook and chat.

Ingredients
8 sea bass fillets
200 g long grain rice
400 ml water
1 tsp lemon juice
about 3 tbsp olive oil, plus extra
    for frying the plantain
1 green plantain, cut into 1 cm slices
handful of plain white flour
salt and pepper

For the salsa:
1 red onion, sliced
juice of 3 lemons
pinch of salt
handful of curly parsley, chopped
1 plum tomato, sliced, deseeded
    and juice reserved
1 green pepper, cored, deseed
    and sliced
olive oil

To serve:
lettuce leaves
1 avocado, sliced,

1. Sprinkle the sea bass fillets with salt and pepper and leave them to stand while you prepare the other ingredients. Wash and drain the rice 3 times under cold running water and place in a small pan. Add the water, a pinch of salt and the lemon juice. Bring it to the boil, then reduce the heat and add 1 tablespoon of oil. Simmer for 5–8 minutes until the rice is tender and the water has been absorbed.

2. Pour enough oil into a small frying pan to give a depth of 2 cm and heat it over a medium-high heat. Add the plantain slices and fry. When they are golden but not completely cooked through, remove them from the pan. Press down on them with a metal spatula and then return them to the pan until completely cooked and crisp. Remove them from the heat and keep warm.

3. Coat the seasoned sea bass fillets in a handful of flour, dusting off any excess. In another frying pan, heat 1–2 tablespoons of oil over a medium-high heat. Add the sea bass, cover the pan and cook for 2–3 minutes, or until the flesh flakes easily; remove from the pan and keep warm.

4. Make the onion salsa by sprinkling the sliced red onion with the lemon juice and salt and set aside. Mix the parsley with the onions, tomato and pepper. Add a little oil and the reserved tomato juice to make a lush salsa.

5. To serve, put the rice in a dish and arrange a layer of lettuce over it; place the fish on top and serve the salsa alongside. Accompany with the cooked plantain and avocado.

Servings: 4
Level of difficulty: Intermediate
Preparation time: 25 minutes
Cooking time: About 30 minutes

I loved the way Rocio fried and crushed the plantain. I think this was a winner because it's such a fresh and exotic way to cook fish.
Paul

PAUL'S CHOICE

JOLOFF RICE WITH LAMB
BY AYODELE SCOTT

1. Mix 2 tablespoons of chopped thyme and 2 tablespoons of tomato purée together and combine with the cubes of lamb, rubbing well into the meat, then season the lamb mixture with salt and pepper to taste. Heat half the oil in a large flameproof casserole over a medium heat. Add the lamb in batches and fry until brown, then set aside.

2. Heat the remaining oil in the same pan. Add the onion and chilli and fry for about 5 minutes, or until the onion is softened. Stir in the remaining tomato purée, then add the red onion, peppers, rosemary and the remaining thyme and continue frying, until the vegetables are soft. Stir in the lamb with any remaining tomato purée and thyme mixture. Cover the casserole, reduce the heat to low, and leave the lamb to cook for 1–2 hours until tender.

3. Towards the end of cooking, prepare the basmati rice. Wash it in running water, then drain and put it into a pan with the water and olive oil. Bring to the boil, then reduce the heat to low, cover the pan and simmer gently for 12–15 minutes until the rice is tender and the water has been absorbed. While the rice is cooking, heat enough oil for shallow frying in a large frying pan. Add the potato slices, fry, turning once or twice, until golden and cooked. Stir the potatoes into the lamb. To serve, spoon the rice on to a serving plate and pile the lamb on top.

Ingredients
3 tbsp chopped thyme
3 tbsp tomato purée
675 g boneless lamb shoulder, cubed
4–6 tbsp olive oil
1 onion, chopped
1 chilli, deseeded and chopped
2 red onions, chopped
2 peppers, green and orange, cored, deseeded and chopped
1 tbsp chopped rosemary
oil, for shallow frying
5 floury potatoes, such as Maris Piper, parboiled and sliced
salt and pepper

For the rice:
400 g basmati rice
600 ml water
1 tbsp olive oil

Servings: 4–6
Level of difficulty: Intermediate
Preparation time: 30 minutes
Cooking time: Up to 2 hours 30 minutes

This recipe comes all the way from Sierra Leone, and Ayodele is so enthusiastic. Putting the fried potatoes in at the end is a very interesting idea.
Paul

HERDWICK LAMB, DAMSON AND JUNIPER PIE
BY CAROLINE WATSON

1. Make the pastry first. Sift the flour into a mixing bowl and rub in the butter with your fingertips until the mixture resembles fine breadcrumbs. Stir in the dry mustard and just enough cold water to bring the mixture together into a soft dough. Turn this on to a lightly floured board and knead it lightly until smooth, then form it into a ball. Wrap it in cling film and put it in the fridge while you make the filling.

2. Preheat the oven to 170°C / gas 3. Heat the oil in a frying pan over a medium-high heat. Brown the lamb in batches and transfer it to a large flameproof casserole. Add the onion and swede to the frying pan and cook until softened and turning golden, then stir them into the lamb. Add all the remaining filling ingredients to the casserole and top it up with as much water as needed to cover. Cover with a lid and put in the oven for 2 hours (or simmer over a low heat) until the meat is tender. Remove the casserole from the oven or hob and allow it to cool.

3. An hour before you want to serve, preheat the oven to 170°C / gas 3. Take the dough out of the fridge, allow it to warm up a little and then roll it out on a lightly floured board. Use two-thirds to line a large pie dish and fill this with the lamb mixture. Cover the lamb with the remaining dough and crimp the edge to seal. Brush the beaten egg over the top to glaze. Cut a small hole in the top to allow the steam to escape during baking. Put the pie dish on a baking sheet and bake for 40 minutes, or until the pastry is golden.

Ingredients

For the shortcrust pastry:
500 g plain white flour, plus extra
    for dusting
230 g salted butter, diced
1 tsp dry mustard
beaten egg, to glaze

For the filling:
1–2 tbsp oil
1 kg Herdwick hogget or other
    boneless lamb shoulder, cubed
4 onions, chopped
1 swede, chopped
600 ml stout or ale
100 g black pudding, chopped
200 g damsons, stoned
1 tsp juniper berries, ground
1 small jar of damson jam
½ tsp dried garlic
½ tsp ground ginger
½ tsp ground cinnamon
1 tbsp Hawkshead relish
    or Worcestershire sauce

You cook this nice and slowly – this pie is really delicious – and red cabbage would be the perfect autumnal accompaniment.
Antony

Servings: 6
Level of difficulty: Intermediate
Preparation time: 30 minutes
Cooking time: Up to 2 hours 40 minutes

ANTONY'S CHOICE

WELSH LAMB DINNER

BY MARILYN MONTEITH

Ingredients

For the lamb:
700 g boneless Welsh leg of lamb, diced
1 tbsp olive oil
1 small onion, finely chopped
1 garlic clove, finely chopped
2 large potatoes, peeled and thinly sliced
300 ml lamb stock
2 tsp cornflour

For the marinade:
1 tbsp olive oil
1 tsp balsamic vinegar
1 tsp English mustard
1 tbsp chopped mint
pinch of dried herbes de Provence

For the leeks:
2 large leeks, sliced and rinsed
1 garlic clove, finely chopped
1 tbsp snipped chives
1 tbsp olive oil

For the mash:
900 g carrots, diced
450 g parsnips, diced
450 g swede, diced
salt

For the vegetables:
1.4 kg new potatoes, scrubbed
1 sweetheart cabbage, shredded
½ a large Savoy cabbage, shredded
salt and pepper

1. Put the lamb in a mixing bowl. Whisk together all the marinade ingredients and pour them over the meat, then stir well to ensure the pieces are coated evenly. Cover the bowl and leave the lamb to marinate for 30 minutes at room temperature.

2. For the leeks, put the leek slices in a shallow ovenproof dish. Mix together the garlic, chives and olive oil. Pour this mixture over the leeks and stir, then cover the dish with foil; set aside.

3. Now assemble the lamb dish. Heat the oil in a large frying pan over a medium heat. Add the onion and garlic and fry them together, stirring for 2 minutes before adding the lamb; scrape in any marinade and meat juices which have accumulated in the bowl. Continue frying for a further 15 minutes, or until the meat is browned.

4. Preheat the oven to 180°C / gas 4. Roughly scatter the potatoes over the bottom of a medium flameproof casserole, keeping enough to one side to use as a top layer. Put the lamb mixture on top of the potatoes, pour over the stock and cover with the remaining potato slices. Put the lid on the casserole and place it, and the dish containing the leeks, in the oven. Roast for 1 hour.

5. Meanwhile, prepare the vegetable mash. Put the carrots, parsnips and swede in a large pan, cover them with water, add a little salt and bring to the boil. Partially cover the pan and boil for 10 minutes, then reduce the heat, simmer for a further 40 minutes, or until very tender.

6. While they are cooking, prepare the accompanying vegetables. Cut any of the larger new potatoes in half and then put all of them in a pan. Cover with cold water, add a pinch of salt, bring to the boil and cook for 20 minutes, or until tender. Place both the cabbages in a steamer and steam them over the potatoes as they cook.

7. Remove the lamb casserole and leeks from the oven and tip everything into a large saucepan. Mix the cornflour with a little cold water to form a smooth paste, add it to the lamb and cook over a medium heat, stirring well as it thickens. Leave it simmering gently while you finish off everything else.

8. Put the leeks into a frying pan over a high heat and fry them for about 2 minutes until browned. Drain the root vegetables and mash them together thoroughly, then drain the new potatoes. Season all the vegetables to taste. Tip all of the vegetables into warmed serving dishes and serve them with the lamb.

Servings: 4–6
Level of difficulty: Intermediate
Preparation time: 30 minutes, plus 30 minutes marinating
Cooking time: 1 hour 20 minutes

Good hearty fare, nice and warming on cold winter days — just what you want from comfort food.
Antony

WINNER

LUCY'S HOG AND DOUGH
BY ELLEN LINFORD

Ingredients

350 g white self-raising flour,
  plus extra for dusting
175 g reduced-fat shredded suet
900 g–1.1 kg pork leg joint
little sunflower oil, for drizzling
18 small potatoes, scrubbed
  and halved
6 parsnips, halved
6 plain pork sausages
2 large onions, sliced
600–850 ml beef stock
salt and pepper

This recipe came from my grandmother, who was a really keen cook. She used to make Hog and Dough for her father and brothers, having it ready for when they got in from work. It was a really useful dish because it was economical – you could use cheaper cuts of pork if necessary – and it could be left in the warming tray of the range. I think it's unique to Northamptonshire, where the men would build up hearty appetites working on the land or in the shoe factories, but the way this version is made is probably unique to my grandmother. This goes well with steamed Savoy cabbage, and for me the perfect accompaniments are mustard or home-made apple sauce and gravy made from the pan juices.

1. Preheat the oven to 200°C / gas 6. Grease a deep-sided roasting tin or ovenproof dish and set aside. Mix the flour, suet and salt in a bowl, then stir in enough cold water to make a soft dough. Make sure you combine these ingredients lightly so that the resulting pastry is light too. Wrap the dough in cling film and place it in the fridge to chil.

2. Put the pork in the prepared tin or dish and drizzle over a little sunflower oil, then roast it for 30 minutes. Meanwhile, put the potatoes and parsnips in a pan of salted water and cover, then bring it to the boil and cook for 5 minutes. Drain and put to one side. Cook the sausages in a frying pan until they are browned all over. Remove them from the heat and set aside.

3. Take the meat out of the oven and add the potatoes, parsnips and sausages, together with the sliced onions, and arrange them around the joint. Pour the stock over the top, adding enough to cover the vegetables, and season with salt and pepper.

4. Remove the dough from the fridge and divide into 4 equal portions. Roll out the portions on a lightly floured surface into 4 strips which are long enough to cover the length and width of the tin or dish. These strips should be about 4 cm in width, but that depends on the size of the container. Dampen the edges of the tin or dish with water and lay the strips over the edges, making sure the pastry is wide enough to cover the vegetables and sausages, while leaving the joint uncovered in the centre.

5. Return the tin or dish to the oven and bake for a further 30–35 minutes, or until the meat, vegetables and pastry are all cooked. The cooked pastry should be crisp on the top and more 'doughy' underneath. If you find that the pastry is browning too quickly during cooking, cover the tin loosely with foil.

6. Remove the pork from the tin and leave it to rest, covered, in a warm place for 15 minutes, then carve the joint and serve each portion with the vegetables, a sausage and a portion of pastry.

Servings: 6
Level of difficulty: Intermediate
Preparation time: 25 minutes
Cooking time: 1 hour–1 hour 5 minutes.

*This is an extraordinary dish and I wasn't sure
I would like it – but it really came up trumps.
Antony*

WINNER

PORK VINDALOO
BY MIGNON JOHNSON

This is a traditional Goan dish, and nothing like as hot as the version often encountered here. I'm passionate about cooking authentic Indian food and have eaten lots of 'Western' Indian food in the UK, but the quality is generally nowhere near as good as it is in India. I like to give people the chance to taste Indian food as it should be. My mother taught me to cook; sometimes I was allowed to help, but usually I just observed what she did. This dish came from her, in a collection of handwritten recipes. It is good served with plain basmati rice and, ideally, a lentil dish. The curry leaves, which have a citrus scent, lend a distinctive curry aroma to the dish, and are fried to release their flavour. You will find them in some supermarkets and most Asian food shops. If you buy more than you need, they can be kept in the fridge in a sealed plastic bag for a week.

1. First, marinate the meat. Place the pork cubes in a non-metallic bowl and add the garlic and ginger pastes, pepper, salt, turmeric, chilli powder, malt vinegar, cumin and mustard powder. Stir well to ensure the pork is coated, cover the bowl and leave to marinate overnight in the fridge.

2. When you are ready to cook the vindaloo, heat the oil over a medium heat in a large saucepan or flameproof casserole with a tight-fitting lid. Add the onion and fry, stirring frequently, for about 8–10 minutes, or until browned. Then add the curry leaves and the marinated pork, along with any remaining marinade, and cook, stirring, until the meat is browned; you may need to add a little water if it looks too dry. Add the hot water, cover the pan and leave to simmer for 30 minutes, or until the pork is tender.

Ingredients
1 kg boneless leg of pork, cubed
½ tsp garlic paste
1 tsp ginger paste
½ tsp black pepper
1 tsp salt
1 tsp ground turmeric
1 tsp chilli powder
3 tbsp malt vinegar
1 tsp ground cumin
1 tsp mustard powder
2 tbsp vegetable oil
1 large onion, finely chopped
20 curry leaves
300–400 ml hot water

Servings: 4-6
Level of difficulty: Easy
Preparation time: 20 minutes, plus
overnight marinating
Cooking time: 45 minutes

Incredible. Marinating the pork overnight is vital because you want good depth of flavour.
Antony

WINNER

GUYANESE PEPPERPOT
BY JONATHAN PHANG

My parents fell in love in Guyana but their families disapproved and my mother was sent to Britain, where she arrived knowing no one. However, my father followed her and they were married over here. I learned to cook from my mother, and food really bonded our family together. Pepperpot is Guyana's national dish but everyone has their own version – it can even get competitive between individual members of a family. The smell of it cooking is really evocative, bringing back happy memories – and particularly memories of my mother, who has passed away. Very little effort is required to make this chilli-hot stew – it practically cooks itself, and the slow-cooked pig's trotters give the dish extra richness. Cassereep, which gives this its distinctive bittersweet flavour, comes from the juice of cassava root. You'll find it in Caribbean food shops as well as some wholefood shops. For an authentic touch, serve it with boiled white rice.

1. Heat 2 tablespoons of groundnut oil in a large pan or flameproof casserole set over a medium-high heat. Add the pork, beef and pig's trotters in batches and fry, setting them to one side as the batches are browned. Add extra oil to the casserole if neccessary. Return all the meat to the pan, season with salt and pepper and cover with water. Bring to the boil, then reduce the heat to low and simmer for 1 hour, skimming as necessary.

2. Add the cassereep, cinnamon stick, sugar, hot pepper sauce, Scotch bonnet chillies, cloves, thyme sprigs and dried thyme to the pan. Bring the Pepperpot back to the boil, then reduce the heat, re-cover the pan and simmer for 1–2 hours until the meat is tender, adding more water if it looks like drying out.

Ingredients
2–3 tbsp groundnut oil
450 g boneless pork shoulder, chopped
450 g lean stewing beef, chopped
3 pig's trotters, chopped
100 ml cassereep (see introduction)
1 x 4 cm cinnamon stick
2 tbsp demerara sugar
2 tsp hot pepper sauce
2 Scotch bonnet chillies, finely chopped
  (remove the seeds if you wish)
6 cloves
3 thyme sprigs
1 tsp dried thyme
salt and pepper

The flavours of this dish are seductive and intriguing; it's not for the faint-hearted but it's worth the effort to go to a fine butcher and track down the trotters.
Paul

Servings: 6
Level of difficulty: Easy
Preparation time: 20 minutes
Cooking time: Up to 2 hours 30 minutes

ANTONY'S CHOICE

BACON AND CABBAGE WITH CHAMP AND PARSLEY SAUCE
BY NORAH BROWN

1. Put the bacon joint in a large, heavy-based pan with the bouquet garni, onion and carrot. Cover with boiling water and return to the boil, skimming the surface, then reduce the heat and simmer for 30 minutes. Lift the joint out of the water and set aside; reserve the water.

2. Preheat the oven to 220°C / gas 7. Combine the honey, sugar and butter, and brush over the meat. Place it in a roasting tin and bake for 10 minutes, or until browned. Take the joint out of the oven and allow it to rest for another 10 minutes. Slice the joint and cover the slices with foil; return them to the oven for 5–10 minutes to finish cooking.

3. To make the cabbage ramekins bring the bacon cooking liquid to the boil. Remove the thick ribs from the green leaves of the cabbage – the leaves should be in 2 halves – and blanch the leaves in the bacon water for 1 minute. Remove, allow them to cool and pat dry. Line 4 buttered ramekins with the cabbage leaves, making sure you have a good overhang. Finely shred the white part of the cabbage and blanch in the bacon water too. Drain and keep warm.

4. Melt the butter in a heavy-based frying pan. Add the onions and mushrooms and fry for 3–4 minutes until lightly browned. Season with a little pepper, but no salt. Add the shredded cabbage and cook for 1–2 minutes. Spoon this mixture into the ramekins and fold the overhanging cabbage leaves over. Place the ramekins in a roasting tin filled with enough boiling water to come halfway up their sides, and put the tin in the oven.

5. Now make the parsley sauce. Melt the butter in a heavy-based pan over a low heat. Add the flour and cook, stirring, for a few minutes. Add the milk and whisk until boiling, then whisk in the parsley and season.

6. Cook the carrot batons with the sugar in boiling water for 6–7 minutes, until tender. Drain and tie them in neat bundles using the blanched chives; keep warm.

7. To make the champ, bring the cream to a simmer with the spring onions and cook for a few minutes; set aside. Cook the potatoes in boiling salted water until they are soft; drain and return to the pan to dry out over a gentle heat. Then mash them, adding the spring onion mixture and beating it in well.

8. To serve, place the ham slices down the centre of an oval platter. Turn out the cabbage ramekins (seam side down) on one side and place the carrots on the other. Put 2 large spoonfuls of champ at each end. Pour the parsley sauce along the middle of the ham.

Ingredients
900 g quick-cook bacon joint
1 bouquet garni
½ an onion, studded with 6 cloves
1 carrot, quartered
1 tbsp clear honey
1 tbsp demerara sugar
15 g butter, melted

For the cabbage ramekins:
½ large Savoy cabbage
15 g butter , plus extra for the ramekins
1 onion, finely chopped
100 g brown cap mushrooms,
  wiped and finely chopped
freshly ground black pepper

For the parsley sauce:
50 g butter
50 g plain white flour
600 ml milk
4 tbsp chopped curly parsley

For the carrots:
1 large carrot, cut into batons
1 tsp sugar
8 chives, blanched and cooled

For the champ:
75 ml single cream
4 spring onions, finely chopped
4 large potatoes, peeled and quartered

Servings: 4
Level of difficulty: Intermediate
Preparation time: 30 minutes
Cooking time: About 1 hour 25 minutes

I love the idea of blanching the cabbage in the bacon water. This is drop-dead gorgeous Irish food and it's lovely.
Antony

WINNER

BAKED HAM WITH COLA

BY JENNIFER MIDDLETON

I love entertaining and like quirky recipes that surprise people; this one is my favourite as it reminds me of my childhood. I'm from the USA, and originally came to Britain on a scholarship to Cambridge. I grew up in Minneapolis; though my father was a Lutheran minister it was actually a Jewish neighbourhood, and I learnt to cook from my first boss at a bagel factory. This is the way my mother used to do ham; she was from Atlanta, where Coca-Cola is made.

1. Put the gammon into a large, heavy-based pan with the onion, a few cloves, the cinnamon stick and orange quarters. Carefully pour the cola over the ham. Bring to the boil, then reduce the heat, cover and simmer for 2½ hours until it is cooked through and tender. Remove from the heat and allow the meat to cool a little in the pan.

2. Heat the oven to 240°C / gas 9. Remove the ham from the cooking liquid and put it in a roasting tin. Now take most of the fat off the meat, leaving only a thin layer. Score this into diamond shapes using a sharp knife and stud with the remaining cloves. Mix the maple syrup, mustard and brown sugar together and spread the mixture over the ham. Put it into the oven and roast for 10 minutes until the ham is glazed.

3. For the potato salad, place the potatoes in a pan with 2 teaspoons of salt. Add enough water to cover them and bring to the boil, then cover the pan, reduce the heat and simmer for 15 minutes, or until the potatoes are soft. Meanwhile, fry the bacon in a heavy frying pan over a medium heat until crisp. Using a slotted spoon, transfer the bacon to kitchen paper to drain; leave the bacon fat in the pan.

4. Drain the potatoes. When they are cool enough to handle, peel them and cut into slices 5 mm thick. Place these in a large bowl and crumble in the bacon.

5. Put the frying pan containing the bacon fat over a medium heat. Add the spring onions and cook for 3–4 minutes. Stir in the cornflour, sugar, the remaining half teaspoon of salt and add pepper to taste. Increase the heat slightly, add the vinegar and bring to the boil, stirring constantly. Pour this dressing over the potatoes and stir them together gently. Garnish with watercress. Slice the ham and serve it with the potato salad.

Ingredients

2 kg mild-cure gammon joint
1 large onion, quartered
handful of cloves
1 cinnamon stick
1 orange, quartered
2 litres cola (not a diet version)
2 tbsp maple syrup
2 tsp English mustard
2 tbsp brown sugar

For the potato salad:
6 potatoes, unpeeled
2½ tsp sea salt
4 streaky bacon rashers,
  rinds removed if neccessary
1 bunch of spring onions, chopped
2 tbsp cornflour
2 tbsp sugar
black pepper
65 ml vinegar
watercress sprigs, to garnish

Servings: 8
Level of difficulty: Easy
Preparation time: 30 minutes
Cooking time: About 3 hours

This fantastic baked ham in coke, which originated in Atlanta 'the home of Coca-Cola', both looks and smells lovely.
Antony

PAUL'S CHOICE

ROAST ROLLED PORK WITH BUTTERNUT SQUASH
BY SARAH THATCHER

1. Preheat the oven to 190°C / gas 5. Heat the olive oil in a large frying pan over a medium-low heat. Add the onion and fry, stirring occasionally, for about 8–10 minutes, until soft; leave it to cool slightly, then add the sage.

2. Unroll the pork loin and cover the inside surface with the onion and sage mixture, then roll it up again and tie securely with string. Weigh the joint to confirm the exact weight. Place the meat in a large roasting tin and roast for 25 minutes per 450 g.

3. Meanwhile, cook the potatoes in a large pan of boiling salted water for 5 minutes. Drain them well and add to the roasting tin when the pork still has about an hour to cook; you may need to add a few spoonfuls of olive oil. Then add the squash and carrots to the roasting tin and return it to the oven. Continue cooking until the vegetables are tender and the pork is cooked through and the juices run clear when you pierce it with knife. Remove the pork and vegetables from the oven, take them out of the roasting tin and leave the meat to rest for 10 minutes before serving; keep the vegetables warm.

4. While the pork is resting, make the gravy. Strain the meat juices out of the roasting tin into a pan. Stir in the scrumpy or cider, vegetable stock and mustard. Mix the flour to a paste with a little cold water and stir it into the gravy. Boil, stirring, until the gravy has thickened, then put it into a warmed jug or gravy boat. Carve the meat and serve it with the roasted vegetables and the gravy.

Ingredients

2 tbsp olive oil plus extra for
   the roasting tin (optional)
1 onion, chopped
handful of fresh sage, chopped
1.5 kg free-range rolled loin of pork
5 potatoes, peeled and cut into chunks
1 butternut squash, skinned and
   cut into chunks
5 carrots, coarsely chopped

For the gravy:
200 ml scrumpy or cider
200 ml vegetable stock
2 tsp wholegrain mustard
1 tbsp plain white flour

This is how roast pork should be, and the cider in the gravy gives it a lovely sweet, aromatic note.
Paul

Servings: 4
Level of difficulty: Intermediate
Preparation time: 25 minutes
Cooking time: About 1 hour 30 minutes

NIGERIAN RICE AND STEW

BY GRACE KERRY

1. Put the lamb and chicken in a large saucepan along with one of the onions and half the herbs. Pour over enough water to just cover everything, season it with a little salt, and bring to the boil. Reduce the heat and simmer for 20 minutes, or until almost all of the water has evaporated.

2. Blend the tomatoes in a blender or food processor with the remaining herbs, red pepper and as much of the Scotch bonnet chilli as you want, depending on how hot you like your food – bearing in mind that these chillies are as hot as they get!

3. Heat the oil in a large saucepan over a medium heat. Add the second onion and garlic, and fry, stirring occasionally, for about 5 minutes, or until golden and softened. Add the blended tomatoes, the stock cube and chilli powder, cover and simmer for 5 minutes. Add the cooked meat along with its stock, stir gently, cover and simmer very gently for another 20 minutes.

4. Meanwhile, put the rice in a bowl with water to cover and leave to soak for 10 minutes.

5. Drain the rice in a sieve and rinse it with fresh water. Tip it into a large saucepan, pour in enough hot water to come 2.5 cm above the rice and add a pinch of salt. Bring the water to the boil, then reduce the heat, cover the pan and leave to simmer for 10–15 minutes until the rice is tender and all the water has been absorbed. Top the water up as it cooks if necessary.

6. While the rice is cooking add the salmon to the stew and cook for a final 10 minutes until the stew has thickened and the oil has settled on the top. Finally, fluff up the rice with a fork and serve it alongside the stew with a sprinkling of fresh coriander.

Ingredients

6 lamb cutlets
6 free-range chicken thighs or drumsticks
2 onions, chopped
2 coriander leaves
2 basil leaves
sprig of thyme
400 g can plum tomatoes
1 red pepper, cored, deseeded
   and chopped
1 Scotch bonnet chilli, deseeded
   and roughly chopped
100 ml vegetable oil
1 garlic clove, finely chopped
1 vegetable stock cube, crumbled
1 tsp medium or hot chilli powder
450 g basmati rice, to taste
3 small salmon fillets, cut in half
salt
chopped fresh coriander, to garnish

This simple, full-flavoured dish has an appealing chilli kick – a hearty stew that celebrates comfort cooking.
Antony

Servings: 6
Level of difficulty: Easy
Preparation time: 10 minutes
Cooking time: About 1 hour

WINNER

CUMBERLAND TOAD IN THE HOLE
BY AUSTEN DAVIES

Juicy tomatoes, field mushrooms and fresh parsley give a modern twist to my version of this traditional British classic. I'm a small-scale pig farmer, specialising in rare breeds. I love pigs and enjoy making such dishes as black puddings and faggots, as well as traditional sausages. I'm passionately against factory farming. Using something you've produced yourself is very special; you know the animal has had a good life. I'm also the Chairman of the Cumberland Sausage Association, and feel strongly about the importance of local food. I really like cooking, and sitting down and eating together as a family is very important to us.

Ingredients
150 g plain white flour
4 free-range eggs, lightly beaten
150 ml whole milk
2 tbsp olive oil
8 Cumberland sausages
6 field mushrooms, wiped and sliced
1 large tomato, sliced
2 tbsp finely chopped parsley

1. Prepare the batter at least 2 hours in advance. Place the flour in mixing bowl, make a well in the centre and pour in the eggs together with a little milk. Beat well, gradually bringing the flour into the centre and adding the remaining milk as you go, until you have a smooth batter; leave it to rest.

2. Preheat the oven to 170°C / gas 3, and cook the sausages. Heat the olive oil in a large non-stick frying pan over a medium heat. Add the sausages and fry until browned on all sides. Pour any fat from the pan into a roasting tin. Place the sausages on the rack over the tin and roast in the oven for 10 minutes.

3. Lift the rack and sausages off the roasting tin and increase the oven temperature to 200°C / gas 6. Lay the tomato and mushroom slices in the tin and roast them in the oven for 5 minutes.

4. Stir the parsley into the batter. Take the roasting tin out of the oven and put the sausages on top of the mushroom and tomato slices, then pour over the batter. Return the tin to the oven for a further 30–40 minutes until the batter is well-risen and golden.

Servings: 4
Level of difficulty: Easy
Preparation time: 10 minutes, plus 2 hours resting for the batter
Cooking time: About 1 hour

Austen follows an unusual method for making this Toad, but it works and it really impressed the judges.
Antony

WINNER

CARIBBEAN CHICKEN AND CHICKEN LIVER STEW
BY LUNA FRANK-RILEY

I'm originally from Trinidad. I first made this dish when I came to the UK as a student to remind me of home cooking. In Trinidad stews were always cooked on Sundays, and you'd make this one to impress your boyfriend, to show him you could really cook. I suggest serving this with steamed mixed vegetables such as baby sweetcorn, broccoli and carrots.

1. Place the chicken pieces in a shallow non-metallic dish. Squeeze the lemon juice over the chicken, then sprinkle with salt and leave for 2 minutes. Thoroughly rinse away all the lemon juice and salt, drain the chicken pieces, and return them to the dish; set aside.

2. Place the onion, garlic, thyme leaves, pepper and ketchup in a food processor or blender and process to a paste. Spoon half the paste over the chicken pieces, rubbing it in well, then cover the chicken and leave to marinate in a cool place for 30 minutes. Add the remaining paste to the chicken livers, making sure the livers are well coated. Cover and leave them to marinate in the fridge for 20 minutes.

3. Put half the oil and half the sugar in a large heavy-based pan (ideally cast-iron) set over a medium heat. Stir until the sugar has dissolved and is beginning to caramelise. Continue heating, watching carefully, until the mixture turns a beautiful chestnut colour. Add the chicken pieces and stir until they are coated with the caramelised sugar.

4. Reduce the heat to low and add enough boiling water to just cover the chicken, then crumble in the stock cubes, stirring. Add the Scotch bonnet, being careful not to cut or puncture it – just allow it to float in the pan. Cover the pan and bring the mixture slowly to the boil, then simmer for 35–40 minutes until the chicken is cooked through and tender.

5. Meanwhile, in a separate heavy-based pan, repeat the caramelisation process for the chicken livers, using the remaining oil and sugar. Once the chicken livers have been added to the caramelised sugar, add a few tablespoons of boiling water, bring the mixture back to the boil, reduce the heat and simmer for 2–3 minutes, or until the livers are just tender (do not overcook them).

6. Add the chicken livers to the chicken mixture, then stir in the creamed coconut and soya milk; take care not to damage the whole pepper. Bring the liquid back to the boil, then reduce the heat and simmer for 10 minutes. Remove the pepper using a slotted spoon and serve the stew.

Ingredients
500 g chicken legs and thighs (about 6 mixed legs and thighs in total), skinned
juice of 1 lemon
1 tbsp salt
1 onion, chopped
2 garlic cloves, chopped
leaves from 4 sprigs of thyme
1 tsp black pepper
2 tbsp tomato ketchup
500 g chicken livers, cleaned
4 tbsp sunflower oil
4 tbsp demerara sugar
2 chicken stock cubes
1 Scotch bonnet chilli or other similar small, fresh, sweet chilli pepper (whole, with stalk)
1 tbsp grated creamed coconut (from a solid block)
3 tbsp soya milk

Servings: 6
Level of difficulty: Advanced
Preparation time: 25 minutes, plus 30 minutes marinating time
Cooking time: About 1 hour 10 minutes

This is really unusual, but it's stunning – definitely one of my favourites.
Antony

WINNER

STUFFED CHICKEN, BABY COURGETTES AND VINE LEAVES
(DJAJ MAA KOUSSA WARAK ENAB)
BY AMOUL OAKES

I'm in heaven when I'm in the kitchen, and this recipe is special because it was given to me by my mother, who was a wonderfully creative cook, and it reminds me of my home in Lebanon. I think love is the most important ingredient in any dish. No one else cooks it exactly this way . To complete the Middle Eastern feast serve this with a bowl of tabbouleh, a salad dressed with garlic and lemon, and goat's yogurt mixed with cucumber, garlic and mint.

1. Put the rice in a bowl. Add the minced lamb and mix together with your fingers, adding the salt, cinnamon, pepper and vegetable oil; set aside.

2. Core the courgettes, removing their centres and taking care not to break them. You need to be able to fill them with some of the stuffing, so they have to be quite empty. Spoon in some of the stuffing, leaving a 2 cm gap at the top – the stuffing will expand as it cooks.

3. Place the vine leaves in a heatproof bowl and cover with boiling water to remove any excess salt, then carefully take them out and put them in a colander to drain. One by one, lay them apart on a board. Position each leaf with the stem side up; carefully remove the stem. Place a little of the stuffing (reserving about half for the chicken) across the leaf, in a line no thicker than 1 cm and leaving 1 cm at each end. Fold the leaf in from both sides, bringing it over the stuffing, and roll it from the top to the bottom, to make a tight, compact, cigar-shaped roll. Put half of these in a large flameproof casserole, enough to fit snugly in one layer.

4. Rub the chicken with the lemon and a sprinkling of salt, inside and out. Combine the nutmeg, cinnamon, coffee and pepper and rub the chicken with this mixture, inside and out again.

5. Mix the pine nuts with the remaining stuffing and then fill the cavity of the chicken. Secure the open end of the chicken with toothpicks, or use a needle and thread to prevent the stuffing from escaping. Place the chicken in the casserole, breast down, on top of the vine leaves. Scatter over the cardamom pods. Cover the chicken with the stuffed courgettes and with the remaining stuffed vine leaves.

6. Pour in enough water to cover the contents of the pan and add the unsalted butter, salt and lemon juice. Put a plate or lid on top of everything to keep the vine leaves in place and bring the liquid to the boil. Reduce the heat to very low, cover, and gently simmer for 3–4 hours, until the vine leaves on top are tender and almost all the water has been absorbed. If there is still some liquid left, don't worry. Tip everything into a bowl and serve.

Ingredients

For the stuffing and vegetables:
800 g Egyptian rice or pudding rice, rinsed
1 kg minced lamb
3 tbsp salt
2 tsp ground cinnamon
¼ tsp black pepper
3 tbsp vegetable oil
15 white baby courgettes
1 jar of Californian vine leaves (approximately 18) preserved in brine, rinsed

For the chicken:
1.5 kg chicken
¼ lemon
½ tsp freshly grated nutmeg
½ tsp ground cinnamon
½ tsp finely ground coffee, preferably Lebanese or Turkish
¼ tsp ground black pepper
100 g pine nuts, roasted with 15 g unsalted butter
4 green cardamom pods
3 tbsp unsalted butter
1 tsp salt
juice of 1 lemon

Servings: 6
Level of difficulty: Advanced
Preparation time: 45 minutes
Cooking time: Up to 4 hours

Here are the genuine flavours of the Middle East, and though this dish is a lot of work it's substantial and incredibly satisfying to do.
Paul

WINNER

LILY KWOK'S CURRY
BY HELEN TSE

I am third-generation British Chinese. This curry recipe comes from my grandmother Lily, and uses spices she collected at the ports where the boat stopped on her journey to Britain from Hong Kong. She was the first woman to open a Chinese restaurant in Manchester, which is now run by my twin sister – my mother used to run it, too. I'm very close to my grandmother; we go on weekly shopping trips and through them I learn a lot about my heritage and family history. Our family all get together and have dinner once a week – food really unites us.

1. Start by making the sauce. Heat the oil or ghee in a heavy-based pan or wok over a high heat. Add the onion and stir-fry for 3 minutes, or until starting to soften but not brown. Add the ginger, garlic and chillies and continue stir-frying for 30 seconds, then reduced the heat to very low and leave to cook, stirring occasionally, until the onion is softened but nothing browns.

2. Stir in the turmeric, cumin, coriander, chilli powder and curry powder and continue cooking very gently for a further 5 minutes. Don't burn the spices or the sauce will taste acrid; sprinkle on a few drops of water if you're worried. Remove the pan from the heat and allow the mixture to cool a little.

3. Put the water in a food processor or blender and add the contents of the pan. Blend until everything is very smooth, then add both the flours and blend again. Put the puréed mixture back into the pan and simmer for 20–30 minutes (the longer the better) over a very low heat, stirring occasionally. Add a little hot water if it starts to catch, but the idea is to gently 'fry' the sauce so that it darkens in colour to an orangey brown. Once you have a thick paste, gradually stir in the stock and simmer until the curry sauce has reduced.

4. Now prepare the chicken. Season the cornflour with salt and pepper to taste, and toss the chicken strips in this to coat them. Heat the oil in a large frying pan over a high heat. Add the chicken pieces and stir-fry for a couple of minutes until they turn white. Add the onion and peas and stir-fry for a further few minutes, then stir in the curry sauce and heat until everything is piping hot. Serve immediately.

Ingredients
For the sauce:
6 tbsp vegetable oil or clarified butter
3 onions, finely chopped
4 cm piece of fresh ginger,
   peeled and thinly sliced
4 garlic cloves, sliced
4 mild fleshy red chillies, deseeded
   and chopped
½ tsp ground turmeric
½ tsp ground cumin
½ tsp ground coriander
½ tbsp chilli powder
2½ tsp curry powder
125 ml water
2½ tsp plain white flour
2½ tsp self-raising white flour
400–500 ml chicken or vegetable stock

For the chicken:
3–4 tbsp cornflour
2 boneless, skinless chicken breasts,
   cut into strips
2 tbsp vegetable oil
½ an onion, thinly sliced
2 tbsp of shelled peas
salt and pepper

Servings: 2
Level of difficulty: Easy
Preparation time: 20 minutes
Cooking time: About 1 hour

If you're used to Indian curries, this one will be a bit different —normally curries are more of a braise, but this has clear, fresh tastes. It's a great family curry.
Paul

PAUL'S CHOICE

GARLIC KARAHI CHICKEN
BY SAADIA USMANI

You won't want to go out for a curry after you try this very easy version. It's excellent served with warm naan bread, or zeera (cumin) basmati rice, and raita.

1. Heat the oil in a wok with a lid over a medium heat until it is fairly hot. Add the onion and stir-fry until golden brown. Add the chicken pieces and fry until they are browned. Add the garlic, tomato purée and tomatoes. Increase the heat to high and continue stir-frying for 2–3 minutes.

2. Reduce the heat to low, cover the wok, and leave to simmer for 10 minutes, or until the chicken is cooked through and tender and the mixture has changed to a deeper colour. By this time, oil should be visible on the surface around the edges of the mixture. Stir in the chilli and coriander, replace the lid and simmer for a further 10 minutes or so.

3. Season with salt and serve.

Ingredients

3 tbsp sunflower oil

1 onion, chopped

1 kg boneless, skinless chicken thighs and legs, diced

5 garlic cloves, finely chopped

2 tsp tomato purée

400 g can of chopped tomatoes

1 large green chilli, deseeded and finely chopped

small bunch of coriander, chopped

¼ –½ tsp salt, to taste

This straightforward dish is right up my street, I love big flavours like these – and lots of garlic.
Paul

Servings: 4–6

Level of difficulty: Easy

Preparation time: 15 minutes

Cooking time: About 25 minutes

ROAST CHICKEN WITH BACON AND MARMITE
BY FLOSSIE SQUIRES

Perk up Sunday lunch with this new twist on roast chicken. Serve it with steamed green vegetables for a great family meal.

1. Preheat the oven to 190°C / gas 5, and spread a thin layer of Marmite all over the chicken. Squeeze the lemon half into the chicken cavity, then gently ease back the breast skin – take care not to pierce the skin – and squeeze lemon juice over; this gives the chicken more flavour. Stuff the cavity of the chicken with the herbs and garlic, then cover the breast with the bacon rashers. Place the chicken in a roasting tin and roast for 1 hour 30 minutes, removing the bacon after 1 hour; reserve it and keep warm if you want to serve it with the chicken.

2. Meanwhile, make the potatoes. Put the potatoes in a large pan with the onions and bring to the boil. Remove the pan from the heat and drain the potatoes and onions, but reserve about 50 ml of the cooking water. Place the potatoes and onions in another tin, pour the reserved cooking water over them and then dot with butter. Put them in the preheated oven for 45–60 minutes; until they are tender. Serve the chicken with the potatoes and onion, and accompany with the bacon.

Ingredients

1.2 kg free-range or organic chicken
1 tsp Marmite
½ lemon
1 bunch mixed fresh herbs
3 garlic cloves, crushed
6 bacon rashers

For the potatoes:
1 kg floury potatoes, such as Maris Piper, peeled and cut into chunks
2 onions, halved
75g butter

A lovely way of cooking chicken and the Marmite really worked; everything comes together and it lifts the flavour.
Antony

Servings: 4–6
Level of difficulty: Intermediate
Preparation time: 20 minutes
Cooking time: 1 hour 30 minutes

WINNER

PASTA WITH MEATBALLS AND TOMATO SAUCE
BY FRANCESCA CONTINI

I'm obsessed with food, either with thinking about what I've just eaten or what I'm going to eat. I'm fourth generation Scottish Italian, and from a very large Italian family – our kitchen was always full of passion, and sometimes tears if the pasta was overcooked. This dish is always served by my family as the first course on Christmas Day, and I remember helping my mother and my grandmother prepare it. It reminds me of the whole house being festooned with ribbons of drying pasta.

Ingredients

For the meatballs:

250 g minced beef (or 125 g minced pork and 125 g minced beef)

3 tbsp dry breadcrumbs

1 tbsp freshly grated Parmesan cheese

1 tbsp finely chopped flat-leaf parsley

½ an onion, finely grated

1 tbsp raisins

1 large egg yolk, beaten

salt and pepper

For the tomato sauce:

3–4 tbsp extra virgin olive oil

1 onion, very, very finely chopped

1 piece of dried chilli (peperoncino)

1 garlic clove, thinly sliced

3 x 400 g tins of Italian plum tomatoes, blended and sieved to remove seeds

1 tbsp finely chopped flat-leaf parsley

For the home-made egg pasta:

300 g 00 Italian durum wheat flour, plus extra for dusting

2 large organic eggs

3 large organic egg yolks

parmesan cheese shavings, to serve

1. Make the meatballs first. Combine the minced meat, breadcrumbs, Parmesan cheese, chopped parsley, onion and raisins in a large bowl. Add the egg yolk and mix it in with a fork or clean hands, then season with salt and pepper. Form the mixture into 6–9 small balls and set aside.

2. Now make the tomato sauce. Heat the oil in a large pan, over a medium heat. Add the onion and fry, stirring, for 5 minutes, or until softened. Add the dried chilli to flavour it, then add the garlic and cook until soft. Pour in the tomatoes and gently put the meatballs in the sauce. Cover the pan and cook over a very low heat for 1–2 hours, leaving the pan lid balanced on a wooden spoon to let some steam evaporate. Towards the end of cooking, add the flat-leaved parsley and adjust the seasoning, if necessary.

3. Meanwhile, make the pasta. This will take about an hour the first time, but will get quicker the more you do it. Put the flour in a large bowl. Make a well in the centre and break the eggs in to it, adding the yolks as well. Using a fork, whisk the eggs into the flour gradually and the mixture will become denser and form into a ball; stirring everything together at once may result in too dry and crumbly a mixture that won't form a dough. Use your hands to press the dough together; try to let it take in as much flour as it's comfortable to handle. This stage can also be reached using a food processor with the dough attachment. Add more flour if the dough is too sticky.

4. Put the dough on a floured work surface and knead it with the palms of your hands. Push it away from you, constantly folding it over, rotating it 90 degrees and kneading again. Keep working the dough until it becomes smooth and elastic, dusting it with a little flour if it gets at all sticky. It is ready when you can ease it apart between your hands to show a smooth, silky surface with no cracks. Cover it with cling film and allow it to rest for 30 minutes.

CONTINUED ON PAGE 88

CONTINUED FROM PAGE 86

5. Divide the dough into 6 pieces. Take one and leave the others covered. Attach a pasta machine to a table at a comfortable height and pass the dough through its widest setting. Fold it equally into three (fold the narrowest side a third of the way along the length of the dough and then fold it over again, keeping the edges tidy so it is easy to work with). Pass the even, folded edge through the rollers again and continue to roll and fold at the widest setting about eight times. At some point you may get a noise like bubble-gum popping as an air pocket is forced through the rollers; this means the dough is ready. Don't worry if you don't hear this; the dough will also look silky smooth.

6. Now start to thin out the dough. Reduce the width of the setting on the pasta machine and pass the dough through so that it becomes thinner and longer. It should not be sticky, but add a sprinkling of flour if it is. Don't fold it any more, just pass it through each reduced setting. It should be thin and fine, but not too fine to handle.

7. When the dough is in a fine strip, let it dry for a few minutes before cutting it. One way to do this is to suspend a broom between two chairs and drape the pasta over the handle – put greaseproof paper over it, and on the floor below, before putting the pasta on. Prepare the rest of the dough in the same way.

8. Cut the pasta into tagliatelle using the narrower of the two cutters on a standard pasta machine, being careful to catch the strips at the other end; the cut pasta can then be hung to dry a little over the broom handle. Cook it in plenty of boiling, salted water for about 4 minutes; it is done when it floats to the surface. Drain well and serve with the tomato sauce and meatballs. Garnish with parmesan cheese shavings.

Servings: 2 generous portions
Level of difficulty: Advanced
Preparation time: 1 hour 20 minutes, plus
30 minutes resting for the pasta dough
Cooking time: Up to 2 hours

This very lovely pasta with tomato sauce and meatballs is something of a family heirloom. It's delicious.
Antony

FILLET STEAKS WITH WHISKY CREAM
BY SUE PARKER-ROBERTS

This dish, showcasing the best of Scotland, is particularly good served with steamed carrots and baked new potatoes.

1. Heat the olive oil and soya butter in a large heavy-based frying pan over a medium-high heat. Add the steaks and fry until they are done to your liking – medium will take about 6 minutes. Remove them from the pan and keep them warm while you make the sauce.

2. Add the onion to the pan and fry, stirring often, for 5 minutes, or until soft. Pour in the red wine and boil, stirring occasionally and scraping up all the bits from the base of the pan until the liquid is reduced by half. Stir in the mustard and season with salt and pepper. Pour in the stock, followed by the whisky and bring the sauce to a simmer. Stir in the soya cream and parsley. Adjust the seasoning if neccessary.

3. Serve the steaks smothered in sauce.

Ingredients

2 tbsp olive oil
1 tbsp soya butter or soya margarine
2 x 175 g fillet steaks
1 onion, diced
60 ml full-bodied red wine, such as Shiraz
1 tbsp wholegrain mustard
150 ml chicken stock
50 ml whisky
100 ml soya cream
handful of freshly chopped curly parsley
salt and pepper

This recipe is ideal for anyone with dairy intolerance, and you can always substitute dairy equivalents if you are not.
Paul

Servings: 2
Level of difficulty: Easy
Preparation time: 20 minutes
Cooking time: 15 minutes

WINNER

LOUISIANA FLANK STEAK GUMBO
BY SINN LOUIS

I'm from the USA and meals were always interesting when I was growing up; with my father being Afro-Caribbean and my mother Cherokee, there were many unusual dishes. I worked in a bank, and this recipe comes from a wonderful elderly client. She would invite the staff to bring the ingredients over, and she'd cook the gumbo – but never revealed the recipe. One day she asked me to visit. She told me that she was the last woman in her family, the recipe had been passed down through generations – and she'd chosen me to keep it going. She died two weeks later. I serve this dish with wild rice and crusty brown bread on the side.

Ingredients

1.1 kg flank steak (or skirt),
  cut into strips about 6 x 2.5 cm
10 boneless chicken thighs, skin on
1–2 tbsp Creole seasoning
1–2 tbsp Cajun seasoning
1–2 tbsp garlic granules
plain white flour, for dusting
sunflower oil, for frying
400 g hot and spicy sausages,
  ideally Polish Wieska ring sausage,
  cut into 3 cm pieces
3 x 400g cans of chopped tomatoes
200 ml chicken stock
2 bay leaves
450 g white fish fillets, such as
  haddock or cod
½ celery stick
2 sprigs of thyme
350 ml milk
white pepper
3 tbsp caster sugar
10–20 okra, trimmed and cut in half
  lengthways
10 crab claws
900 g large peeled prawns, uncooked
2 red chillies, finely chopped
2 large onions, thinly sliced
3 large green peppers, sliced into rings
salt and pepper

Servings: 10–12
Level of difficulty: Intermediate
Preparation time: 25 minutes
Cooking time: About 1 hour 40 minutes

1. Season the steak and chicken thighs with half the Creole and Cajun seasonings, garlic granules and salt and pepper. Toss the steak strips in a little flour to coat the pieces all over, shaking off any excess.

2. Heat 3 tablespoons of oil in a large flameproof casserole or pan over a medium-high heat. Stir-fry the strips of steak in batches for 3–4 minutes, or until they are browned all over, adding a little extra oil with each batch, if necessary. Remove them from the casserole using a slotted spoon and set them aside. Sear the chicken in the same casserole, browning the pieces on both sides. Once they start to colour, add the sausage pieces and fry until the chicken is crisp and the sausage browned. Then return the steak to the casserole.

3. Stir in the tomatoes, stock and bay leaves and heat gently, stirring, until the mixture is almost boiling. Reduce the heat, cover the casserole and leave to simmer, stirring occasionally, for about 30 minutes, or until the meat and chicken are tender.

4. Put the fish fillets in a frying pan, skin side down, and add the celery and thyme. Pour the milk over them and sprinkle with salt and white pepper. Cover the pan and heat gently until the liquid is barely simmering. Poach the fish for about 3 minutes until it is just cooked. Transfer it to a plate and put it to one side; discard the poaching liquid.

5. Now go back to the casserole. Stir in the remaining Creole and Cajun seasonings, or add enough to taste, then stir in the sugar. Add the okra and simmer for 5 minutes. Crack the crab claws, scoop out the meat, and add it to the casserole; if you're short of time, you could just crack the claws and add them to the pan with the shells more or less intact.

6. Remove the skin from the poached fish and flake the fish over the top of the casserole, then scatter the prawns and chillies over the top as well. Put the lid on the casserole again and simmer for 5 minutes, then cover the surface of the gumbo with the onion slices and green pepper rings but don't stir them in.

7. Reduce the heat to very low, cover the casserole once more and simmer for another 5 minutes. Discard the bay leaves before serving.

Dishes from the Deep South are always packed with great tastes, and here's an excellent way of using a cheaper cut of meat.
Antony

WINNER

NOT ENTIRELY TRADITIONAL GUINNESS STEW
BY DOMINIC CAULDWELL

My great passions in life are playing the guitar and food, and I often combine the two by cooking for my band after rehearsals. I began cooking when I was at university and realised that good food wasn't going to fall out of the sky! I'm half Irish, half Chinese, and my Chinese mother originally altered this Guinness stew to include more oriental flavours. I started making it about five years ago, but she's been doing it for ages. She's a very good cook and we all like to eat together as a family on a regular basis. Serve this with a mound of mashed potatoes and a steamed green vegetable, such as beans or broccoli.

Ingredients

3 tbsp plain white flour
1.5 kg braising steak, cut into 5 cm cubes
3–4 tbsp vegetable oil
 or 45–60 g of butter
2 onions, chopped
6 garlic cloves, chopped
1 cm piece of fresh ginger, peeled
 and thinly sliced
4 carrots, chopped
1 can of Guinness
500 ml beef stock,
 or canned luxury beef consommé
3 tbsp dark soy sauce
150 g chestnut mushrooms,
 wiped and halved
salt and pepper
bunch of flat-leaf parsley, finely chopped,
 to garnish

1. This dish can be cooked either in the oven or on the hob, over a low heat. If you want to use the oven, preheat it to 150°C / gas 2. Season the flour generously with salt and pepper and toss the beef cubes in the seasoned flour. Heat half the oil or butter in a heavy-based flameproof casserole over a fairly high heat. Add the beef and brown in batches; set aside as they are done.

2. Reduce the heat. Add more oil or butter to the casserole if necessary and gently cook the onion, garlic and ginger for 10 minutes, or until softened. Add the carrots and cook for a further 2 minutes. Pour in the Guinness and beef stock or consommé, then return the browned beef to the casserole and add the soy sauce. Cover the casserole and simmer it over a very low heat, or cook in the oven, for at least 2 hours, or until the meat is meltingly tender.

3. Heat the remaining oil or butter in a frying pan. Add the mushrooms and fry, stirring until golden, then add them to the casserole. Taste and add more soy sauce if needed. Garnish with finely chopped parsley and serve.

This is a beautifully dark and rich stew; a special take on a classic with an interesting cultural twist.
Antony

Servings: 6
Level of difficulty: Easy
Preparation time: 25 minutes
Cooking time: Up to 2 hours 30 minutes

WINNER

RABBIT STEW

BY ANDREW NAYLOR

I'm a sculptor and sculpture conservationist, and I was restoring the Waterloo Memorial in Belgium when I tried a traditional rabbit stew made with Belgian fruit beer. When I returned I decided to try my own version (I do a lot of the cooking at home), using local ale and rabbits from a friend who is also a butcher. This recipe has echoes of the simple country food of my childhood and it enables me to use local ingredients – the pub in our village brews its own beer. It also reminds me of the good friends I made in Belgium. You'll really enjoy this served with creamy mashed potatoes with spring onions stirred in.

Ingredients

4 tbsp olive oil
2 wild rabbits, jointed
4 rashers of dry cured bacon,
   cut into 1 cm strips
150 g Milano salami, chopped
600 ml bitter beer
200 g carrots, cut into chunks
4 celery sticks, cut into chunks
300 g shallots, halved
   or quartered if large
2 tsp Dijon mustard
2 bay leaves
2 garlic cloves, finely sliced
1 cm piece of fresh ginger, peeled
   and finely chopped
150 g sultanas
1 tsp plain white flour – mashed with
   1½ tsp softened butter – optional
salt and pepper

1. Preheat the oven to 150°C / gas 2, and heat half of the oil in a large ovenproof casserole over a medium heat. Once it is hot, add the pieces from one of the rabbits and brown them all over. Remove them from the dish, heat the remaining oil and repeat with the second rabbit, then remove that one too. Add the bacon and salami to the casserole and fry them until golden brown.

2. Return the rabbit to the casserole, lower the heat and add the beer. Add the carrots, celery, shallots, mustard, bay leaves, garlic, ginger and sultanas and bring to the boil, stirring once or twice. Reduce the heat until the liquid just simmers, then cover the casserole, put it in the oven and cook for 3 hours.

3. Check the casserole just before serving and if you think the gravy is a little thin, thicken it gradually adding the flour mixed with the butter. Slowly add this to the sauce, mixing well between each addition, checking as you go. Taste for seasoning and serve.

Servings: 6–8
Level of difficulty: Easy
Preparation time: 10 minutes
Cooking time: 3 hours 30 minutes

If you're bored with chicken, then bring back the rabbit for a real country taste.
Antony

PARTRIDGE WITH CIDER, BRANDY AND APPLES

BY DIANA TEMPERLEY

Together with my husband Julian, I farm 150 acres of apple orchards in Somerset, and I cook a lot with our produce – we have cookers and eaters as well as cider apples – as it is so fantastic to cook with food which is right on our doorstep. I often swap apples with a neighbour in return for game birds from his land, and this dish is good with pheasant too. I'm the mother of Alice Temperley, who is a well-known designer, and every year we host a star-studded party in the orchards.

1. Melt the butter in a large, heavy-based flameproof casserole over a medium heat. Add the partridges and apples and gently cook until they are both browned; remove the apples and set aside. Now add 1 tablespoon of the brandy to the pan and carefully ignite it, using a long match. Once the flame disappears, return the apples to the pan, pour in the cider and bring to the boil. Reduce the heat, cover the casserole and simmer for 15 minutes, or until the meat is tender. Remove the partridge and apples from the pan and keep them warm.

2. Bring the contents of the pan to the boil and cook steadily until reduced by two-thirds. Stir the cream, the remaining brandy and soaked raisins into the cider sauce. Return the partridge and apples to the pan, to heat through, and serve straight away.

Ingredients

50 g butter
4 small partridge
5 Bramley or Cox apples, peeled, cored and chopped
75 ml brandy
425 ml cider
125–175 ml double cream
50 g raisins, soaked in 4 tbsp brandy

This uses good seasonal ingredients and local produce. Partridge can be really good value, too.
Antony

Servings: 4
Level of difficulty: Intermediate
Preparation time: 20 minutes
Cooking time: About 20 minutes

PAUL'S CHOICE

HUNTER'S DISH WITH SPICED RED CABBAGE

BY CORNELIS JELIER

1. Melt a knob of butter with the water in a saucepan over a medium-high heat. Add the cabbage, cloves and apples, cover the pan with a tight-fitting lid and leave to simmer for 45 minutes. Check it during this time and make sure it isn't catching, and add a little more water if necessary.

2. While the cabbage is cooking, prepare the hunter's dish. Preheat the oven to 190°C / gas 5 and grease an ovenproof casserole; set it aside. Heat a large knob of the butter in a frying pan, over a medium-high heat. Add the onions and apples and fry them gently, stirring occasionally, until they are golden brown.

3. Set aside enough potato slices to create a final top layer. Arrange alternate layers of the remaining potato slices, the cooked meat, and the onion and apple mixture in the prepared casserole, seasoning between each layer. Pour the stock into the casserole, then arrange the reserved potato slices in a final layer over the top, covering everything completely. Dot the potato slices with the remaining butter, then put the casserole into the oven and bake, uncovered, for 25–30 minutes, or until hot and browned on top.

4. Finish the cabbage just before serving. Stir in the remaining knob of butter, sugar, and vinegar, if using, and simmer for a further 5 minutes. Serve alongside the baked hunter's dish.

Ingredients

For the cabbage:
2 knobs of butter
275 ml water
1 small red cabbage, about 450 g, cored and shredded
3 cloves
2 cooking apples, peeled, cored and sliced
1 tbsp light soft brown sugar
dash of malt vinegar, optional

For the hunter's dish:
75 g butter
3 onions, thinly sliced
225 g cooking apples, peeled, cored and sliced
12 potatoes, boiled, cooled and sliced
750 g cooked meat, such as pork left over from a roast, sliced
salt and pepper
275 ml chicken stock, hot

Servings: 4
Level of difficulty: Easy
Preparation time: 20 minutes
Cooking time: About 55 minutes, plus time to cook and cool the potatoes

A terrific way to use any left-over roast, and the taste of the pork really comes through. I loved its simplicity.
Paul

VENISON EN CROUTE
BY ELSPETH MCNAUGHTON

This makes an impressive dinner party dish when served with parsnips, carrots and new potatoes tossed in olive oil, fresh rosemary, garlic and salt.

1. Make the pastry first. Place the flour and butter in a food processor and mix until blended and crumbly. Add the egg and process until you have a ball of smooth dough; wrap this in cling film and put it in the fridge for 1 hour.

2. Preheat the oven to 200°C / gas 6. Heat a heavy-based frying pan over a high heat until it is very hot. Add the roe fillet and brown for 2 minutes on each side. Season it with salt and pepper and set it aside. Melt the butter in the same pan over a medium-high heat and fry the mushrooms and shallots until they are soft. Crumble in the haggis and add the sage and thyme. Cook this mixture for a few minutes, before adding the gin. Remove the pan from the heat and leave it to cool. Put the roe fillet on a board and spread the cooled mixture on top.

3. Roll out the chilled pastry dough on a lightly floured board into a piece about 2 mm thick and slightly longer – about 5 mm – than the length of the fillet; it should be wide enough to go around it. Dampen the edges of the pastry with milk and carefully put the fillet in the centre. Bring the long edges of the pastry up on top of the fillet and wrap it like a parcel, sealing the pastry well; seal the ends together. Roll the pastry-covered fillet over so that the long join is underneath. Use any dough trimmings to decorate the top and brush with milk.

4. Place the pastry-wrapped fillet on a baking tray and roast for 25 minutes until the pastry is browned. Remove from the oven and leave to rest for 10 minutes before slicing and serving.

Ingredients

For the pastry:
225 g plain white flour,
    plus extra for dusting
115 g unsalted butter, diced
1 egg
milk, for glazing

For the filling:
400 g roe deer fillet
25 g butter
115 g chestnut mushrooms,
    wiped and finely chopped
2 small shallots, finely chopped
75–115 g haggis, preferably a
    venison haggis, casing removed
25 g fresh sage, finely chopped
25 g fresh thyme, finely chopped
2–3 tbsp gin
salt and pepper

Gorgeous, and venison is better for you than other red meats – low in fat and cholesterol.
                                                    Antony

Servings: 3–4
Level of difficulty: Intermediate
Preparation time: 25 minutes, plus 1 hour
chilling for the dough
Cooking time: About 40 minutes

PAUL'S CHOICE

BEEF GOULASH (BOGRACSGULYAS)

BY TOMI KOMALY

1. Heat the oil in a large, heavy-bottomed pan with a lid over a medium-low heat. Add the onions, peppers, garlic and salt and fry, stirring occasionally for 10–15 minutes until the onions are translucent. Meanwhile, with a fork, pierce the skin of each tomato 4 or 5 times and put them in a bowl of boiling water for 2 minutes. Lift them out with a slotted spoon, remove their skins, and chop finely.

2. Add the tomatoes and caraway seeds to the pan and stir for 2–3 minutes until the tomatoes are soft, then add the paprika and cook for a further minute. Now add the beef cubes and cook for another 2–3 minutes. Add enough boiling water to cover the contents of the pan, cover with a lid and simmer the goulash for 30 minutes. Add the potatoes and continue to simmer over a low heat until the meat and potatoes are cooked and the liquid has thickened.

Ingredients
60 ml vegetable oil
200 g onions, finely chopped
150 g green or yellow peppers, cored, deseeded and finely chopped
1 garlic clove, finely chopped
1½ tsp salt
150 g tomatoes
pinch of caraway seeds
1½ tbsp Hungarian or Austrian paprika
750 g lean stewing steak, cubed
1 kg potatoes, peeled and diced

Servings: 4
Level of difficulty: Easy
Preparation time: 20 minutes
Cooking time: About 1 hour 20 minutes

This goulash is the best I've ever tasted. This type of dish is wonderful for dinner – you can do it ahead and it's still stunning.
Paul

BLUE CHEESE, WHITE GRAPE AND RED ONION TART

BY PAULA RICHARDS

I'm a very keen cook and love poring over recipe books to get ideas, though this particular one was suggested by my sister, who'd been travelling in Goa and eaten a cheese and grape tart. It took me about ten attempts to get it right! I used to be in the music business (I'm a rock chick really), and had to tour. I'm also vegetarian, and this was often problematic when we were on the road, but now I run a B&B in St Ives. It has a restaurant and I cook this tart every other day – people love it. I serve it at room temperature accompanied with a rocket, watercress and walnut salad.

1. To make the pastry, mix the flour and paprika in a bowl, then rub in the butter with your fingers until the mixture has the texture of fine breadcrumbs. Slowly add as much cold water as you need to bring the pastry together into a dough. Wrap the pastry in cling film, then chill it in the fridge for 10 minutes. Preheat the oven to 180°C / gas 4, and lightly grease an 18 cm tart tin with a removable base.

2. Roll the pastry out thinly on a lightly floured surface and use it to line the tart tin. Prick the base a few times with a fork, then cover it with a sheet of baking paper and fill it with baking beans. Bake the pastry case for 20 minutes, or until the pastry is almost baked through. Remove the tin from the oven, and the baking beans and paper from the pastry case.

3. Meanwhile make the filling. Heat the oil in a frying pan over a medium heat. Add the onion and fry, stirring occasionally, for about 5 minutes, or until softened. Put the onion, grapes and Stilton into the pastry shell in layers, finishing with a layer of Stilton, and sprinkle the paprika over the top. Return the tart to the oven for another 10–12 minutes until the cheese has melted and the top is starting to brown. Once the tart is ready, remove from the oven and leave to cool.

Ingredients

For the pastry:

100 g plain white flour, plus extra
    for dusting
½ tsp smoked paprika
50 g unsalted butter, at room
    temperature, diced, plus extra for the tin

For the filling:

1½ tbsp olive oil, for frying
1 red onion, finely sliced
200 g sweet white grapes, halved
350 g Stilton cheese, crumbled
½ tsp paprika

This works beautifully. It's got really big flavours, with the sweetness of the grapes and red onions complemented by the cheese.
Paul

Servings: 4
Level of difficulty: Intermediate
Preparation time: 15 minutes, plus chilling
Cooking time: About 35 minutes

WINNER

GADO GADO

BY YUFRITA SKYNER

I come from Aceh in Indonesia, though I've lived in Scotland for some years. I went to Aceh for my sister's wedding in 2004, and we were all going to a party at the groom's house on Boxing Day when the tsunami struck. I saved one of my sons, and my sister kept hold of the other, and my mother, brothers and sisters also survived. The family house and garden were destroyed, and making this traditional dish reminds me of happier times – we used to help our mother prepare it, sitting under the mango trees in our garden.

Ingredients

For the peanut sauce:
vegetable oil, for deep-frying
250 g shelled raw peanuts
2 garlic cloves, peeled
2 shallots, sliced
3 red chillies, split
400 ml water
50 g palm sugar
2 tbsp vegetable oil
1 garlic clove, finely chopped
2 shallots, finely chopped
165 ml coconut milk
½ cm piece of galangal,
    peeled and grated
3 kaffir lime leaves
3 dried bay leaves
½ tsp tamarind paste
1 tsp granulated sugar
2 tbsp sweet soy sauce
salt
½ tsp dried chilli flakes, optional

For the vegetables:
2 tbsp vegetable oil
200 g firm beancurd (tofu),
    sliced 2 cm thick
150 g carrots, cut into strips
150 g bean sprouts
100 g green beans, cut into 2 cm lengths
½ cucumber, peeled
300 g new potatoes, boiled and
    cut into ½ cm slices
100 g round lettuce, roughly torn

For the garnish:
4 hard-boiled eggs, cut into quarters
1 tbsp roughly chopped flat-leaf parsley
50 g Indonesian prawn crackers
4 shallots, sliced and deep-fried
    until golden

1. Begin by making the peanut sauce. Heat 5 cm of oil in a wok over a medium heat. Add the peanuts and fry them, stirring occasionally, for 2–3 minutes until golden. Remove them from the oil with a slotted spoon and transfer to a plate lined with kitchen paper; leave to cool completely. Fry the whole garlic cloves, shallots and chillies in the remaining oil for 1 minute, then leave them to cool alongside the peanuts.

2. Remove the seeds from the chillies and transfer to a food processor with the garlic, shallots and peanuts and coarsely grind, then add 200 ml of the water and the palm sugar, and blend again until smooth.

3. Heat the 2 tablespoons of oil in a medium pan over a moderate heat. Add the finely chopped garlic and shallots and fry them, stirring continuously for 2–3 minutes until golden brown. Then add the peanut and chilli paste to the pan, together with the coconut milk, galangal, kaffir lime leaves, bay leaves, tamarind paste and the remaining water. Bring the mixture to the boil, stirring occasionally. Reduce the heat and simmer gently until the sauce has slightly thickened. Add the sugar, soy sauce and salt to taste, and the chilli flakes if you like it spicy; set aside.

4. For the vegetables, heat the oil in a frying pan over a medium heat. Season the beancurd slices with salt and fry them for 4 minutes on each side. Transfer these to a plate covered with kitchen paper and leave them to cool.

5. Bring a large pan of water to the boil. Add the carrot strips and blanch them for 2 minutes. Take them out of the water with a slotted spoon, and transfer to a large bowl of iced water. Repeat with the bean sprouts, blanching them for 1 minute, and finally with the green beans, blanching them for 4 minutes. Cut the cucumber in half lengthways, scoop out the seeds with a teaspoon and discard them. Grate the cucumber flesh and set aside. Drain the blanched vegetables.

6. Cut the cooled beancurd into small cubes and arrange on a large serving plate along with the prepared vegetables and cucumber, the boiled potatoes and lettuce. Pour over the peanut sauce and garnish the dish with the hard-boiled eggs, parsley, prawn crackers and deep-fried shallots.

Servings: 4–6
Level of difficulty: Intermediate
Preparation time: 30 minutes, plus 1 hour cooling
Cooking time: About 40 minutes

This is exactly my sort of food, and it's very good.
And what a story to go with this dish
— Yufrita deserves all her luck.
Antony

SWEET THINGS

WINNER

APPLE, BRAMBLE AND CUSTARD BAKE

BY ALAN AIR

This recipe is a tribute to my dear friend Dorothy, who died a few years ago. She had the allotment next to mine – she was thirty years older but we became great friends. She helped me through some rough times and taught me to cook, almost as therapy, and we even won Cumbrian Allotment of the Year together, which was fantastic. The first time I had this dish was at Dorothy's one Christmas, and she used brambles that she had picked in September and frozen.

1. Make the pastry. Sieve the flour and salt into a large mixing bowl, add the lard and butter and rub the fats into the flour until the mixture resembles fine breadcrumbs. Slowly add enough chilled water to shape it into a firm dough and form it into a ball. Wrap it in cling film and chill for at least 30 minutes.

2. Place the prepared apple in a saucepan along with the sugar and 1–2 tablespoons of water. Cook over a low heat stirring until the apple has broken down and has a soft consistency.

3. Preheat the oven to 180°C / gas 4. Lightly grease a 30 cm flan tin with a removeable base. Roll the pastry out on a floured surface and use it to line the dish. Prick the base with a fork, then line it with baking parchment and fill with baking beans. Bake the pastry case 'blind' for 15 minutes, then remove the baking beans and parchment, and bake for a further 5 minutes until golden. Leave it to cool for 10–15 minutes. Spread the cooked apple over the pastry base and layer the blackberries on top.

4. Put all of the custard ingredients, except for the flour, in a large mixing bowl and whisk them together. Sieve the flour into the bowl and whisk again until it is fully incorporated, then put to one side while you make the crumble topping. Rub the butter into the flour until it looks like breadcrumbs, then stir in the sugar. Pour the custard over the fruit in the flan dish, then sprinkle the crumble mix over the top. Place the flan tin on a baking sheet and bake for 30 minutes, until golden brown, and leave it to stand for 10 minutes before serving.

Ingredients
225 g plain white flour,
  plus extra for dusting
pinch of salt
55 g lard, diced
55 g chilled butter, diced
1 large cooking apple, peel, cored
  and chopped
2–3 tbsp granulated sugar
150 g blackberries
double cream, to serve

For the custard:
340 g can evaporated milk
3 free-range eggs, beaten
30 g caster sugar
30 g butter, melted
1 tsp vanilla essence
45 g white self-raising flour

For the crumble topping:
85 g chilled butter, diced
140 g plain white flour
85 g granulated sugar

Servings: 6–8
Level of difficulty: Easy
Preparation time: 30 minutes
Cooking time: About 1 hour

This is a big, gutsy, family-style pudding with a touching story behind it, and could well become one of your standard dishes.
Paul

PAUL'S CHOICE

APPLE AND PLUM CRUMBLE
BY KATHY BURKIN AND JANE WISEMAN, DIPTFORD PRIMARY SCHOOL

1. Preheat the oven to 180°C / gas 4, and grease an ovenproof serving dish about 20 x 28 cm in size and 5 cm deep.

2. Make the filling. Put the apples and plums in the dish, sprinkle the sugar and ground cinnamon over them, then add the water and mix everything together. Bake for approximately 10 minutes. Once the juices are running and the fruit is softened, take the dish out and increase the oven temperature to 200°C / gas 6.

3. For the topping, put the flour, butter and sugar in a food processor and blend until the mixture resembles fine breadcrumbs. Tip the mixture into a bowl and add the porridge oats, stirring them in well; don't add them to the food processor as you want them to remain rough. Spread the topping evenly over the fruit in the dish, and return it to the oven. Bake for about 30 minutes until golden brown and serve with cream, ice cream or custard.

Ingredients

675 g Bramley apples, peeled,
  cored and thickly sliced
675 g Cox's apples, peeled,
  cored and thickly sliced
12 plums, stoned and quartered
25 g light muscovado sugar
1 tsp ground cinnamon
2 tbsp water

For the topping:
280 g white self-raising flour
140 g butter
140 g demerara sugar
70 g porridge oats

cream, ice cream or custard, to serve

Servings: 6–8
Level of difficulty: Easy
Preparation time: 25 minutes
Cooking time: 40 minutes

This crumble is a good combination of fruit and a light, oaty topping, which is delicious.
Paul

PAUL'S CHOICE

SOMERSET CIDER CAKE
BY GILL BULLOCK

1. The day before you plan to bake this, put the sultanas in a bowl, pour the cider over them and stir to mix them together. Cover the bowl and leave the sultanas to soak at room temperature overnight.

2. Preheat the oven to 180°C / gas 4, then grease and line a 24 cm spring form cake tin with greaseproof paper and put it to one side. Cream the margarine and sugar together in a bowl until pale and fluffy, then gradually add the eggs, beating well after each addition.

3. Sift the flour, baking powder and mixed spice together, then fold it into the creamed mixture. Stir in the sultanas and their soaking liquid together with the apples. Transfer the mixture to the prepared tin and level its surface. Bake the cake for between 1 hour 30 minutes and 1 hour 45 minutes until risen and firm to the touch and golden brown.

4. Remove the cake from the oven and leave it to cool in the tin for 20 minutes, before turning out on to a wire rack and cooling.

Ingredients

425 g sultanas
255 ml cider, preferably a local variety
255 g soft margarine
340 g caster sugar
3 eggs, beaten
425 g plain white flour
2½ tsp baking powder
1½ tsp ground mixed spice
340 g cooking apples (prepared weight), peeled, cored and chopped

This would be great with a cup of tea, and you could try making it with pears as well.
Paul

Servings: Makes one 24 cm round cake
Level of difficulty: Easy
Preparation time: 25 minutes, plus overnight soaking
Cooking time: 1 hour 30 minutes to 1 hour 45 minutes

WINNER

BLACKBERRY AND APPLE PIE
BY MARJORIE REEVES

I'm 84 – and as a child I dreamed of owning a tea shop. I started a bakery in 1975, selling sausage rolls, pasties, bread and thirty types of cake. It closed in 1990 but people still stop me in the street to tell me how much they remember the things we sold. I now spend much of my time making cakes and puddings for my grandchildren and great-grandchildren.

1. Make the pastry first, because it needs to chill. Put the flour in a mixing bowl and rub in the butter until the mixture resembles breadcrumbs. Then stir in the sugar, followed by the water. Mix until the ingredients come together to form a ball of dough. Wrap this in cling film and put it in the fridge for at least 30 minutes.

2. Preheat the oven to 200°C / gas 6. Now make the filling. Put the apples in an ovenproof dish with the water and sugar. Bake them for 30–40 minutes until they are tender. Remove the dish from the oven and leave it to cool (the apples could also be cooked in a microwave oven). If they have given off a lot of juice, strain some of it into a bowl and set aside. Turn down the oven to 170°C / gas 3.

3. Put the blackberries in a saucepan with a dash of water and cook over a low heat until they have softened but still hold their shape. Tip the berries into a sieve and catch any juices in a bowl. Combine the apples with the berries and moisten with just enough juice to give a syrupy consistency. Don't discard any extra berry juices – save them for serving with ice cream.

4. Take the pastry dough out of the fridge and roll out two-thirds, on a lightly floured surface. Use this to line a pie dish and spoon in the fruit filling; put a pie funnel into the middle. Roll out the remaining pastry dough into a piece large enough to cover the pie dish. Dampen the edges of the dish and cover it with the dough, letting the top of the funnel poke through. Brush the top with beaten egg and dust it with caster sugar; use any pastry trimmings to make leaves and balls to decorate the pie. Bake for 30 minutes, or until the pastry is cooked and golden, then serve with Devonshire clotted cream.

Ingredients
For pastry:
350 g white self-raising flour,
    plus extra for dusting
175 g butter
115 g caster sugar
80 ml water

For the filling:
900 g Bramley apples, peeled,
    cored and quartered
80 ml water
115 g sugar
450 g blackberries

1 egg, beaten, for glazing
caster sugar for dusting
Devonshire clotted cream, to serve

Apples and blackeberries work really well together and this pie makes a fantastic autumnal treat.
Paul

Servings: 6–8
Level of difficulty: Intermediate
Preparation time: 30 minutes
Cooking time: About 1 hour 10 minutes

PAUL'S CHOICE

AUSTRIAN APPLE STRUDEL
BY MARGARET REES

Ingredients

For the filling:
50 g unsalted butter
100 g fresh white breadcrumbs
1 kg cooking apples, peeled
juice and zest of 1 lemon
80 g white sugar
1 tsp ground cinnamon
1 tsp grated nutmeg
1 tsp ground cloves
50 g raisins, soaked in 1 tbsp rum
50 g flaked almonds, toasted

For the strudel dough:
200 g strong white bread flour,
    plus extra for dusting
125 ml warm water
1 tsp white wine
1 tsp butter
vegetable oil for greasing the baking tray
melted butter, for brushing
icing sugar, for dusting
vanilla custard flavoured with rum,
    to serve

1. Begin by making the filling. Melt the butter in a small frying pan and fry the breadcrumbs until lightly browned. Coarsely grate the apples into a bowl and stir in the lemon zest and juice. Add the sugar, spices, raisins and almonds; set aside.

2. Next make the strudel pastry (you can use a 400 g pack of filo pastry as an alternative). Mix the flour, warm water, white wine and butter together in a warm bowl – it is important that the bowl is kept warm – to form a dough. Turn it out on to a lightly floured board and knead it heavily, banging it on the board until it is silky smooth. Return it to the warm bowl and brush over the surface with melted butter. Cover the bowl and leave it in a warm place for 30 minutes. Preheat the oven to 180°C / gas 4 and lightly grease a large baking tray.

3. You need to use this pastry dough while it is still warm. Turn it out on to a large, lightly floured cotton cloth and gradually work it out to a large rectangle, stretching it softly using floured fingertips. Flour your hands again and slip them, palms down, under the centre of the dough. Working towards the edges, stretch the dough out across the back of your hands until the rectangle is paper thin. Cut off the thick edge with scissors.

4. Sprinkle the fried breadcrumbs all over the pastry, then pile the apple mixture in a strip along the edge of the dough nearest to you. Fold in the side edges of the pastry.

5. Using the cloth to help lift the dough, roll the strudel into a large Swiss-roll shape, starting from the edge with the filling. Press it together firmly. Tuck in the edges to make a neat roll, securing it neatly, and use the cloth to lift the strudel on to a baking tray with a shallow rim. Roll the strudel off the cloth and on to the tray; traditionally apple strudels should be nudged into a large crescent shape. Brush the top with melted butter.

6. Bake the strudel for 45 minutes. After 30 minutes strain off the juices seeping out and drizzle over the pastry. Cover the top with foil if the pastry is browning too quickly. Once it is ready, remove it from the oven, dust with icing sugar and serve warm, accompanied by a thin vanilla custard, flavoured with a little rum.

A proper strudel, the business. Do try making the pastry, but you can always roll puff pastry very thinly and get a good result.
Paul

Servings: 6–8
Level of difficulty: Advanced
Preparation time: 35 minutes, plus resting
Cooking time: About 50 minutes

WINNER

TARTE TATIN
WITH CINNAMON ICE CREAM
BY RACHEL THOMPSON

This is my version of the classic French recipe, using a biscuity pastry rather than the puff pastry used in the original. I now live in Ballymena, where I run a B&B with my husband, but I was born in Armagh, the 'orchard county' of Northern Ireland, where apple dishes were always part of the family menu. I learnt to cook as a small girl with my mother, and now my parents are willing guinea pigs for the dishes I create.

1. Make the ice cream. Heat the cream, milk and cinnamon sticks together in a medium pan until almost boiling, then remove the pan from the heat and leave the liquid to infuse for at least 30 minutes.

2. Using a large mixing bowl, beat the egg yolks, sugar and cornflour together until pale in colour. Pass the infused milk and cream through a sieve and slowly add it to the eggs, stirring well as you go. Return the mixture to a clean pan, and simmer, stirring, over a very low heat until the custard thickens enough to coat the back of a spoon. Leave it to cool.

3. Once it is cool, pour it into an ice cream maker and churn until frozen; the time this takes will vary depending on the type of machine. If you don't have an ice cream maker, pour the mixture into a large shallow freezer container, freeze it for 1 hour, stir it well to break up the ice crystals that have formed, then refreeze. Repeat this 3–4 times until the ice cream is half frozen, then leave it to freeze completely.

4. Now make the pastry for the tarte tatin. Pulse the flour, butter and icing sugar together in a food processor until the mixture resembles fine breadcrumbs. Add the egg, along with some iced water if necessary, to make a ball of smooth dough. Wrap this in cling film and leave it to rest in the fridge for at least 30 minutes.

5. Preheat the oven to 200°C / gas 6. Melt the butter and sugar together in a tarte tatin tin, 23 cm in diameter, over a medium heat and cook for a few minutes until they are a light fudge colour, stirring occasionally. Pack the apples into the tin, arranging them in concentric circles, with their cut sides uppermost. Cover the tin and simmer over a low heat for about 15 minutes, until the apples have softened. Remove it from the heat and leave it to cool slightly.

6. Roll the pastry on a lightly floured surface into a circle a little larger than the tin and put it over the apples, tucking the excess pastry well down the sides. Slash the pastry a couple of times and bake for 20–25 minutes until golden brown. Transfer the ice cream to the fridge for 20 minutes before serving to allow it to soften up enough to scoop, and serve it with the hot tarte tatin.

Ingredients

For the ice cream:
500 ml double cream
500 ml semi-skimmed milk
4 x 2 cm cinnamon sticks, broken
6 free-range egg yolks
100 g caster sugar
1 tsp cornflour

For the pastry:
250 g plain white flour,
　　plus extra for dusting
100 g salted butter, diced
100 g icing sugar
1 free-range egg, lightly beaten
dash of iced water

For the filling:
175 g caster sugar
100 g salted butter
6 dessert apples, peeled, cored
　　and quartered

Level of difficulty: Intermediate
Preparation time: 30 minutes, plus 30 minutes infusing, 5–6 hours freezing for the ice cream and 30 minutes chilling for the pastry
Cooking time: About 1 hour

*Who doesn't love a tarte tatin? And this
one is just right with Rachel's ice cream.*
Antony

WINNER

BORDER TART

BY RACHEL PEARSON

I'm currently putting together a small collection of regional British recipes to keep them alive. This recipe is very important for me not just because it's a traditional Northumbrian dish, but because I was taught how to make it by my mother. We used to have this as a special treat on Sundays (to console us for having to go to school on Monday).

1. Begin by starting the tart filling. Put half the lemon juice and the lime and orange juices in a bowl, add all the grated zest and the sultanas and stir well, mixing everything together. Set aside for 30 minutes until the sultanas have plumped up.

2. Meanwhile, make the almond pastry base. Sift the flour and salt into a mixing bowl, then stir in the ground almonds and sugar. Using your fingertips, lightly rub the butter into the flour mixture until it resembles breadcrumbs. Add the egg and knead the ingredients together until they are well mixed (this behaves more like a biscuit mix than a pastry dough, so it will remain quite crumbly even when the egg has been kneaded in). Cover the bowl and chill it in the fridge for at least 30 minutes.

3. Preheat the oven to 200°C / gas 6 and grease a shallow 24-cm round tart tin with a removeable base. Take the chilled almond pastry out of the fridge. It is virtually impossible to roll it out so simply press it evenly over the base and up the sides of the tin, patching any holes as you go and leaving a little pastry overhanging the top slightly.

4. Place a piece of greaseproof paper over the pastry and cover it with a layer of baking beans to weigh the paper down. Bake for 10 minutes. Remove the baking beans and paper, then return the tin to the oven for 5 minutes. Remove it from the oven once again and trim round the top edge of the tin using a sharp knife, neatly cutting away the overhanging pastry. The almond pastry burns easily, so doing this helps to neaten the edges and improve the appearance of the finished pie.

5. Reduce the oven temperature to 180°C / gas 4 and complete the filling. Put the soaked sultanas and fruit juices in a pan over a low heat and add the butter, ground almonds, walnuts and sugar. Heat them, stirring continuously, until the butter is melted and everything is combined. Remove the pan from the heat and stir in the eggs, mixing well. Pour the mixture evenly into the pastry case. Bake it for 15–20 minutes until the filling is lightly set. Remove it from the oven and put it to one side to cool.

6. While it is cooling, make the lemon glaze by pouring the remaining lemon juice into a small bowl. Sift the icing sugar over the juice and mix it in well to form a smooth, runny glaze. Carefully remove the cold tart from the tin and place it on a serving plate, then drizzle the lemon glaze decoratively over it. Serve the tart in slices, either by itself, or accompanied with crème fraîche.

Ingredients

For the filling:
finely grated zest and juice of 1 lemon
   (preferably unwaxed)
finely grated zest and juice of 1 lime
   (preferably unwaxed)
finely grated zest and juice of 1 orange
   (preferably unwaxed)
150 g sultanas
50 g butter
50 g ground almonds
50 g walnuts, chopped
50 g light soft brown sugar
2 eggs, beaten

For the almond pastry base:
200 g plain white flour
pinch of salt
125 g ground almonds
2 tsp granulated sugar
100 g butter, softened
1 egg, beaten

For the lemon glaze:
50 g icing sugar

Crème fraîche, to serve, optional

Servings: 8
Level of difficulty: Intermediate
Preparation time: 45 minutes – plus soaking time, 30 minutes chilling time and cooling time
Cooking time: 35–40 minutes

A delicious combination, with the almond pastry and the various fruit juices.
Antony

WINNER

GINGERBREAD CAKE
BY JEANNIE GYE

I have severe arthritis and my husband has multiple sclerosis but we believe you can either choose to live or just exist, and I refuse to let my disability keep me from my love of cooking. This recipe was passed to me by my husband's aunt who had been a professional cook, and I've passed it on to my daughter. It's incredibly popular with the family, and my daughter and I fight to eat the crunchy top when it comes out of the oven. You can even serve it as a dessert with custard and more chopped ginger.

1. Preheat the oven to 150°C / gas 2 and line a 1.25 kg loaf tin with baking parchment. Put the flour, ground ginger and mixed spice in a mixing bowl and stir them together. Pour the golden syrup into a pan and add the margarine, lard and sugar; heat gently until everything has melted. Meanwhile, add the egg to the flour and spice mixture and mix it in well. Once the syrup mixture is ready, stir it into the flour mix to make a stiff batter.

2. Heat the milk in a pan until lukewarm and then add the bicarbonate of soda. Add the warm milk to the batter and stir well. If you like, add some thinly sliced stem ginger at this stage, too. Pour the mixture into the tin and scatter finely sliced stem ginger on the top – it must be thinly sliced or it will sink.

3. Bake for 1 hour 30 minutes, or until a skewer inserted in the centre comes out clean – don't open the oven door for at least an hour. Allow the cake to cool in the tin; it can be served either warm or at room temperature.

Ingredients
450 g plain white flour
3 tsp ground ginger
1 tsp ground mixed spice
450 g golden syrup, warmed
55 g margarine
115 g lard
175 g dark muscovado sugar
1 egg, beaten
300 ml milk
1 tsp bicarbonate of soda
3–4 pieces of stem ginger,
 thinly sliced – optional
extra 3 pieces of stem ginger,
 very thinly sliced, for the topping

Servings: Makes 1 large cake, using a 1.25 kg loaf tin
Level of difficulty: Intermediate
Preparation time: 20 minutes
Cooking time: 1 hour 40 minutes

Jeannie obviously has a magic touch with cakes, because this is easily the best gingerbread cake I've tasted.
Antony

PAUL'S CHOICE

CHOCOLATE CAKE

BY JILL BRAND

1. Preheat the oven to 180°C / gas 4. Line the base and sides of a 20 cm springform cake tin with baking parchment.

2. Place the cocoa in a pan and slowly add the boiling water, stirring until smooth. Add the butter and sugar and warm over a low heat until the ingredients have melted together. Remove from the heat and allow the mixture to cool slightly, then gradually add the eggs, beating them in.

3. Sift the flour, bicarbonate of soda and baking powder together and fold into the cocoa mixture. Do this thoroughly until it has an even colour – the mixture will be very sloppy. Pour it into the prepared tin and bake for between 1 hour 45 minutes and 2 hours 15 minutes, until a skewer inserted into the centre of the cake comes out clean. When the cake is baked, remove it from the oven and allow it to cool in the tin for 15 minutes. Then turn it upside down onto a cooling rack and leave it to cool completely. This will give a level finish to the cake.

4. To make the chocolate covering, heat the cream in a pan to boiling point. Remove it from the heat and add the chocolate; stir until it has melted and is blended with the cream. Leave the mixture to cool until it has thickened enough to coat the back of a spoon, then spread over the cake. Put it in the fridge to set before serving.

Ingredients
80 g good-quality cocoa powder
300 ml boiling water
250 g butter
550 g light muscovado sugar
4 eggs, beaten
400 g plain white flour
1 tsp bicarbonate of soda
½ tsp baking powder

For the chocolate covering:
300 ml double cream
400 g dark chocolate, minimum 60%
  cocoa solids, broken into small pieces

*This is a big, rustic chocolate cake
— it really looks the part.*
Paul

Servings: Makes one 20 cm round cake
Level of difficulty: Intermediate
Preparation time: 20 minutes, plus 15 minutes cooling
Cooking time: Up to 2 hours 15 minutes

WINNER

SWISS CARROT CAKE
BY SONJA WATSON

I grew up in South Africa but my parents originally came from Baden, Switzerland – Swiss Germans have a great tradition of baking. I started baking cakes because I didn't really like the ones I found in shops in the UK – they seemed to be about icing and not about the actual cake – so I began making my own from my mother's recipes. I've never altered this one because I take the view that there's no point changing something for the sake of change if it's good already. My mother loved Kirsch and tried to put it in everything!

1. Grease a 22 cm springform cake tin. Whisk the egg whites in a bowl until they are stiff, then set them aside. Mix the egg yolks, sugar and a pinch of salt in another bowl until smooth, and stir in the lemon zest and juice. Add the flour, baking powder, cinnamon, carrots and ground almonds and mix everything together well. Gently fold in the whisked egg whites.

2. Pour the mixture into the cake tin and put it into an unheated oven. Set the oven to 180°C / gas 4, and bake the cake for 50–60 minutes until it is baked through. Test by inserting a skewer into the centre of the cake and removing it; if it comes out clean, the cake is ready. Remove the cake from the oven and allow it to cool in the tin for 10 minutes. Turn it out onto a wire rack to cool completely.

3. Make the icing while the cake is cooling. Sift the icing sugar into a bowl and mix it with the water and kirsch until you have a smooth paste. Pour this on to the cold cake and spread it evenly over the top and sides, using a warm knife. Finally coat the sides and rim of the cake with a 2–3 cm wide band of toasted and chopped almonds.

Ingredients
5 eggs, separated
250 g sugar
pinch of salt
finely grated zest and juice of ½ lemon
100 g plain white flour
1 tbsp baking powder
¼ tsp ground cinnamon
250 g carrots, grated
250 g blanched almonds, freshly ground

For the icing:
200 g icing sugar
1 tbsp water
1 tbsp kirsch
50 g almonds, toasted and chopped

Wonderful. This is rich and moist and it isn't as crumbly as a normal carrot cake.
Antony

Servings: Makes 1 x 22 cm cake
Level of difficulty: Intermediate
Preparation time: 25 minutes
Cooking time: About 1 hour

SUNDAY TEA CAKE
BY PAUL EVANS

1. Preheat the oven to 180°C / gas 4. Using a little butter, grease a baking tin 27 x 18 cm, and about 4 cm deep. Sieve the flour into a large mixing bowl, add the butter and rub it into the flour with your fingertips until the mixture resembles breadcrumbs. Then add the baking powder, a pinch of salt and the sugar.

2. Beat the eggs, milk and sherry together in a jug and then add the liquid to the ingredients in the mixing bowl and mix well. Transfer the cake mixture to the prepared tin and bake for 20–30 minutes, until golden and firm to the touch – a skewer inserted in the centre should come out clean.

3. Remove the cake from the oven and turn it out on to a wire rack. Once cool, cut into squares, dust them with icing sugar and serve with hot custard.

Ingredients
225 g white self-raising flour
100 g chilled butter, diced, plus extra
   for greasing
½ tsp baking powder
pinch of salt
100 g caster sugar
2 large organic eggs
3 tbsp semi-skimmed milk
4 tbsp sweet sherry
icing sugar, for dusting
hot custard, to serve

*This is also good when served fresh from the oven –
delicious with custard. It would also work
with some homemade jam…*
Paul

Servings: 12
Level of difficulty: Easy
Preparation time: 15 minutes
Cooking time: About 30 minutes

WINNER

WINDRUSH-STYLE CARIBBEAN BREAD AND BUTTER PUDDING
BY WENDY MCGUIRE

I've always kept this recipe a secret despite it being so popular with my friends and family – until now! My parents are Jamaican, and food is a very social thing in the Caribbean, it's not just about 'time for dinner, let's eat' but about celebrating life. Whenever I was really good, I was allowed to help my mother make Bread and Butter Pudding – it was comfort food for me and it reminds me of being little. I've adapted her version, given it a more Caribbean twist, made it spicier, and I think it's a perfect fusion dish.

1. Preheat the oven to 180°C / gas 4, and butter a large ovenproof serving dish. Make the breadcrumbs by chopping the slices of bread into crumbs using a food processor. Tip the crumbs into a bowl and stir in the sugar, dessicated coconut, butter and cinnamon. Leave the mixture on one side.

2. Make the custard. Whisk the eggs with the milk, evaporated milk, sugar, nutmeg, cinnamon and mixed spice in a pan over a low heat. Warm the mixture gently, whisking constantly until it has slightly thickened – but don't let it boil or it will curdle. Add the cream and continue whisking until it is thick enough for a wooden spoon to leave a trail when you draw it through the custard. Add the white and dark rums and cook for another minute before removing the pan from the heat.

3. Cut the bread slices in half or quarter, removing the crusts if you prefer, and then butter the pieces generously. Place a layer of buttered bread in the prepared baking dish and cover with some of the soaked raisins, a little of the custard and a sprinkling of coconut breadcrumbs. Then cover that with a little of the custard, a layer of raisins and another layer of buttered bread; press the bread down a little. On the final layer, add the remaining raisins and cover the pudding with custard to ensure that the bread is well soaked. Cover generously with the remaining breadcrumbs and bake for 30 minutes until firm to the touch. Remove the pudding from the oven and drizzle with condensed milk, then return it to the oven for a further 10 minutes until it has risen and is cooked through.

Ingredients

For the breadcrumbs:
6 thick slices of white bread
150 g dark soft brown sugar
75 g dessicated coconut
50 g chilled butter, grated
pinch of ground cinnamon

For the pudding:
3 large free-range eggs, beaten
600 ml milk
400g can of evaporated milk
200 g light soft brown sugar
1 whole nutmeg, freshly grated
pinch of ground cinnamon
½ tsp ground mixed spice
250 ml single cream
1 shot of white rum
1 shot of dark rum
1 large white loaf, a few days old,
    thickly sliced
75 g butter
300 g sultanas or raisins, soaked
    overnight in 50 ml rum and water,
    with a pinch each of ground cinnamon
    and freshly grated nutmeg
1 can of condensed milk

Servings: 4–6
Level of difficulty: Intermediate
Preparation time: 25 minutes
Cooking time: About 1 hour

A gorgeous fusion of British and Jamaican influences. It's so good: the smell, the spices… it is one wicked pudding.
Antony

WINNER

ALMOND RICE
BY MARIANNA ESBENSEN

This is a traditional Danish Christmas dessert, which I've eaten every Christmas Eve – I learnt it from my mother and grandmother. I make it every year, and recently did it for 30 other expatriate Danes. Whoever finds the whole almond hidden inside wins a prize – a child would get a marzipan pig, an adult perhaps a bottle of brandy… but they can't reveal they've won until the end, so they hide it behind their teeth.

1. Put the whole almonds in a bowl, cover them with boiling water and leave to soak overnight.

2. The next day, grease a large saucepan with the butter. Add the rice to the pan, then add just enough water to cover it. Bring it to the boil and boil briskly, uncovered, for 2 minutes. Remove the pan from the heat and stir in the milk, vanilla pod and salt, if using. Return it to a low heat and bring the mixture gently to the boil, then partially cover the pan and simmer for 30 minutes, stirring frequently to prevent the rice from sticking.

3. When the rice is soft and creamy, take the pan off the heat. Carefully remove the vanilla pod (it will be hot!), then gently open it up and scrape the seeds inside back into the rice using a teaspoon. Stir well, then pour the rice mixture into a large bowl and leave to cool completely.

4. Meanwhile, drain the soaked almonds well and pat dry, then slip off and discard the skins (children are good at doing this). Select one large almond and set it aside. Chop the remaining almonds, but not too finely. Lightly toast half of them in a dry frying pan over a low heat for a few minutes, adding the honey, if you wish to use it. Remove the pan from the heat, stir in the remaining chopped almonds and leave them to cool before stirring into the rice mixture. Add the caster sugar (if you are using it) and the vanilla sugar.

5. In a separate large bowl, whip the cream until it resembles soft peaks, then lightly fold into the rice mixture. Transfer the rice to a serving bowl and hide the reserved whole almond somewhere in the middle. Chill it until you are ready to serve.

6. For the cherry sauce, pour the cherries and their syrup into a small saucepan and heat gently until they are almost boiling. In a small bowl, mix the cornflour with 2 tablespoons of water until smooth. Add the cornflour mixture to the cherry sauce and stir over a gentle heat until it thickens. Simmer gently for 1–2 minutes, still stirring, and then add the optional brandy. Pour the cherry sauce into a jug and serve warm alongside the almond rice.

Ingredients

For the almond rice:
200 g whole unblanched almonds
1 tbsp butter, for greasing
220 g short-grain pudding rice
1 litre milk
1 vanilla pod, split lengthways
½ tsp salt, optional
2 tbsp clear honey, optional
2 tbsp caster sugar, optional
1 tbsp vanilla sugar or ½ tsp vanilla extract
500 ml whipping cream

For the cherry sauce:
425 g can of whole black cherries in syrup, pitted
1 tbsp cornflour
2 tbsp brandy, optional

Servings: 6–8
Level of difficulty: Easy
Preparation time: 30 minutes, plus cooling, chilling and overnight soaking
Cooking time: About 55 minutes

*This traditional dish is lovely and simple;
the almond and rice is a super combination,
well complemented by the cherry sauce.*
Paul

PAUL'S CHOICE

BAKEWELL TART

BY CHRISSY ASHWORTH

Ingredients

For the pastry:
100 g plain white flour, sifted
50 g unsalted butter, chilled and diced
1 tbsp caster sugar
1 free-range egg yolk

For the filling:
100 g unsalted butter, softened
100 g caster sugar
2 large free-range eggs, lightly beaten
100 g white self-raising flour
50 g ground almonds
3–4 drops of almond extract
2 tbsp seedless raspberry conserve
handful of fresh raspberries
25 g flaked almonds
crème fraîche, ice cream, cream
   or custard, to serve, optional

1. Make the pastry first. Rub the butter into the flour and stir in the sugar, then the egg yolk and finally add enough cold water to mix everything to a stiff dough. Wrap it in cling film and put it in the fridge for at least 30 minutes to rest. While it is resting, preheat the oven to 190°C / gas 5 and place a baking sheet inside to heat.

2. Prepare the filling by mixing together the butter, sugar, eggs, flour, ground almonds and almond extract in a food processor – or beat them by hand – until smooth. The mixture should have a 'dropping' consistency; if it is a bit stiff add a little milk.

3. Roll out the chilled pastry very thinly and use it to line a 20 cm loose-based metal tart tin, pressing down well with your fingers. Then spread the conserve on top of the pastry and scatter with the fresh raspberries. Finally, pour over the almond filling. Level the surface with a spatula and sprinkle the flaked almonds over the top.

4. Put the tart tin on the hot baking sheet (this ensures the pastry base becomes crisp), and bake for about 25 minutes; check after 20 minutes to make sure it is not browning too fast. When it is done, the filling should yield slightly to your finger. Take the tart out of the oven and let it rest for a short while before removing it from the tin.

5. Serve warm as a dessert with crème fraîche, ice cream, cream or custard. It is also delicious served cold in slices, like a cake, and keeps well for up to a week.

Servings: 4–6
Level of difficulty: Intermediate
Preparation time: 20 minutes, plus 30 minutes resting
Cooking time: 25 minutes

Traditional and straightforward. Bakewell-style tarts like this are among my favourites – they're great with a cup of coffee in the afternoon.
Paul

RICE PUDDING
WITH BOOZY PRUNES
BY DIANE JOHNSON

Both my parents worked seven days a week in Bradford's textile mills, so my grandmother did most of the cooking. This particular recipe conjures memories of her cooking it in the oven of her coal-fired range – it was the most delicious thing I'd ever tasted. I'm passing on her recipes to my grandchildren, just as she passed them to me, and I like to cook this with my granddaughter Jessica. I think it's very important that children should learn to cook properly, and that things don't just come in tins from supermarkets.

1. Preheat the oven to 200°C / gas 6, and generously butter a large ovenproof serving dish.

2. Put the soaked prunes in a pan over a medium heat with the cold tea, Armagnac, water and lemon peel. Bring them to the boil, reduce the heat, and simmer very gently for about 1 hour until the prunes are tender.

3. Once the prunes have started cooking, prepare the rice pudding. Put the pudding rice, milk, sugar and butter into a large pan over a high heat and bring to the boil, stirring constantly. Pour it into the prepared dish and bake for 45 minutes. Serve the rice pudding with the prunes.

Ingredients

450 g dried prunes, stones removed, soaked overnight in 200 ml black tea
100 ml cold black tea
150 ml Armagnac
300 ml water
1 strip of lemon peel
115 g pudding rice
850 ml milk
55 g sugar
15 g butter

I love how simple and traditional this is, it would be great to cook with the kids (well, without the boozy fruit, perhaps – I'd use Bushmills rather than Armagnac there!).
Paul

Servings: 4
Level of difficulty: Easy
Preparation time: 20 minutes, plus overnight soaking for the prunes
Cooking time: About 1 hour

WINNER

ROSE-SCENTED CREAM
BY ERIKA PARRY

I'm a designer for china companies such as Caverswall and Wedgwood and take a lot of inspiration from flowers. I also love cooking with them, and designed a pattern for Aynsley China featuring Rosa gallica, which I often use in the kitchen. I've invented some recipes for my daughter Rozelle's birthday party using roses as a main ingredient.

1. Begin by making the cream. Brush a 1 litre jelly mould lightly with corn or sunflower oil; set aside. Warm a large bowl, pour in the yogurt and crème fraîche and stir until evenly mixed. Whip the cream until it forms soft peaks, then fold it in, along with the sugar. Add a couple of drops of the food colouring – just until it's very pale pink.

2. Put the rose water in a mug, sprinkle the gelatine over, then put the mug in a pan of simmering water and heat until the gelatine dissolves. Remove the mug and mix a tablespoon of the creamy mixture into the gelatine, then quickly fold that mix into the cream. Pour it into the jelly mould and chill in the fridge for 24 hours, until set.

3. Now prepare the rose syrup. Remove the little yellow bit at the end of each rose petal. Put the petals in a saucepan and cover them with cold water, then simmer them over a gentle heat until the petals are soft and wilted. Add the lemon juice – the colour will change immediately to a beautiful pink or red. Transfer the petals and water to a blender and whizz, then return the mixture to the pan. Add the rose water and sugar and stir to dissolve the sugar. Simmer for about 10 minutes or until the syrup thickens slightly.

4. Now prepare the figs and marzipan. Using a fork, mix together the almonds, sugar and enough of the egg white to get a firm and pliable mixture; wrap in cling film. Cut the figs into quarters from stem to base, without cutting all the way through, then squeeze the fleshy sides so the quarters open out like the petals of a flower. Place them under a hot grill for 7 minutes, or until they are slightly charred (you can serve them uncooked if you prefer). Warm the rose syrup and spoon a little over the centre of each fig, catching any that runs off and returning it to the pan. Reheat the syrup if necessary and do this a second time. Divide the marzipan into 6 pieces and roll each one into a small ball. Place a ball in the centre of each fig, pressing the 'petals' in position, then gently press an almond on top.

5. When you are ready to serve, fill a basin with hot water and dip the jelly mould in it for a few minutes. Ease the sides with a knife and turn the cream out on to a glass cake stand. Decorate with a rose; place the figs at the side of the cream and spoon the remaining rose syrup over them. Scatter a few more rose petals and some pomegranate seeds over the dessert and serve.

Ingredients

Corn or sunflower oil, for brushing

For the cream:
450 g Greek yogurt, at room temperature
280 g crème fraîche, at room temperature
284 ml double cream, at room temperature
2 tbsp caster sugar
dash of cochineal food colouring
3 tbsp natural rose water essence
1½ sachets of powdered gelatine

For the rose syrup:
petals from 4 roses, the best red and deep pink scented roses such as Rosa gallica, Zéphirine Drouhin, Rosa centifolia or Roseraie de l'Hay, washed and blotted dry.
juice of ½ lemon
2 tsp natural rose water essence
175 g caster sugar

For the rosy figs and marzipan:
75 g ground almonds
50 g caster sugar
½ egg white, beaten until frothy
6 fresh figs
rose syrup (see above)
6 whole blanched almonds

Servings: 6
Level of difficulty: Intermediate
Preparation time: 45 minutes
(plus setting overnight)

This girlie pud (I hope you like pink) is actually quite posh nosh, but that's not important – it tastes fresh and summery.
Antony

PAUL'S CHOICE

FRUIT DUMPLINGS
BY LADY MILENA GRENFELL-BAINES

1. Push the cheese through a sieve into a mixing bowl, then add the butter, eggs and sugar. Mix them together well, and add the flour, semolina and milk in stages to form a soft, pliable dough. Tip it out of the bowl on to a lightly floured surface, knead it lightly and roll it into a long sausage shape about 6 cm in diameter.

2. Prepare the fruit filling you wish to use. If it's the apricots, then place a square of chocolate in the centre of each fruit to replace the stone and close the halves firmly together. If you have chosen plums, replace the stone with a lump of sugar and close the halves firmly together.

3. Cut a slice of dough about 1 cm thick and put it on a well-floured board. Roll it out into a circle large enough to envelope the apricot or other fruit. Put an apricot or plum on the dough and bring it up around the fruit to enclose it completely. Seal the edges well and repeat with the remaining dough and fillings. If you are using blueberries, use 3–4 per dumpling with a sprinkling of sugar.

4. Bring a large pan of slightly salted water to the boil and drop the dumplings into it, 3 or 4 at a time. Gently move them around the pan with a wooden spoon to ensure they don't stick to the bottom and cook them for 10–12 minutes; they are done when they rise to the surface.

5. Meanwhile, prepare the crumble. Melt the butter in a frying pan over a medium heat. Add the breadcrumbs and fry them gently until golden, then sprinkle in the sugar and stir well. Remove the pan from the heat and tip the crumble mixture into a warmed serving dish.

6. Remove the dumplings as they cook, using a slotted spoon to let them drain. Then roll them in the crumble mixture, and keep them warm in a low oven while you cook the remaining dumplings. Once they are all cooked and coated, serve them hot with the melted butter spooned over, and sprinkled with cinnamon and sugar.

Ingredients

For the dough:
200 g meky tvaroh – a Polish soft cheese
   – or ricotta
15 g butter, melted
2 large free-range eggs, lightly beaten
50 g caster sugar
300 g plain white flour, plus extra
   for rolling out
100 g fine semolina
5 tbsp semi-skimmed milk

For the fruit filling:
500 g apricots or plums, halved and
   stones removed, or whole blueberries
300 g dark chocolate, broken into
   squares (if using apricots)
12 sugar lumps (if using plums)

For the crumble:
40 g unsalted butter
100 g fresh breadcrumbs
2 tbsp granulated sugar

To serve:
15–20g unsalted butter, melted
½ tsp ground cinnamon
3–4 tsp caster sugar

I really loved these, and so did lots of the crew! Absolutely scrumptious; I'm going to try my own version.
Paul

Servings: Makes roughly 20 dumplings
Level of difficulty: Intermediate
Preparation time: 30 minutes
Cooking time: 10–12 minutes per batch

ANTONY'S CHOICE

NORWEGIAN ALMOND CREAM (MANDEL PUDDING)

BY JULES EVANS

1. Lightly grease a 500 ml ring mould; set aside. Put the almonds, sugar and almond essence in a large saucepan over a low heat. Stir in the cream and milk and stir until the sugar has dissolved, then increase the heat. Bring it to the boil and then remove from the heat.

2. Leave the gelatine sheets to soak in a bowl of cold water for 5 minutes to soften them, then squeeze the sheets and place them in a large bowl. Strain the milk mixture over the gelatine and stir until it has melted. Pour the mixture into the ring mould and leave it in the fridge overnight to set.

3. Then make the blueberry compote, which is served with the pudding. Put the blueberries, sugar and water in a pan over a gentle heat and stir to dissolve the sugar, then increase the heat and bring them to a boil. Reduce the heat and simmer for about 5 minutes until the blueberries are soft and mash them with a wooden spoon to help them on their way. Mix the cornflour with a tablespoon of cold water, then stir this into the blueberries. Cook until the compote thickens and remove it from the heat. Sieve it into a bowl, leave it to cool and then chill overnight alongside the pudding.

4. When you are almost ready to serve the pudding, stir the amaretto into the thick cream and scatter it with the almonds. Take the pudding and compote out of the fridge and dip the ring mould in hot water for a few seconds. Tip the pudding out of it on to a serving plate, and accompany it with the blueberry sauce and amaretto cream.

Ingredients

vegetable oil for greasing
85 g ground almonds
115 g golden granulated sugar
1 tsp almond essence
284 ml extra thick double cream
300 ml Jersey milk
4 sheets of gelatine

For the blueberry sauce:
300 g blueberries
115 g golden granulated sugar
125 ml water
1 tbsp cornflour

To serve:
1 tbsp amaretto
284 ml extra thick double cream
1 tbsp flaked almonds, browned

I'm not normally a fan of milk puddings, but the almonds in this one make all the difference.
Antony

Servings: 4–6
Level of difficulty: Easy
Preparation time: 15 minutes, plus overnight chilling
Cooking time: About 10 minutes

PAUL'S CHOICE

SNOW PANCAKES WITH RUM BUTTER

BY JOANNE WILSON

1. Make the rum butter first. Begin by putting the sugar in an earthenware bowl. Warm this in a low oven, or in a microwave. Melt the butter in another bowl, either in the low oven or in a microwave but don't let it start to cook. Once the sugar is warmed, mix in the rum and then carefully add the melted butter, stirring constantly until combined. Beat the mixture until it is creamy and stir in the nutmeg. Pour the mixture into another bowl and allow it to set for 1–2 hours, in a cool place but not in the fridge.

2. For the pancakes, sift the flour and salt into a large mixing bowl. Make a well in the centre of the flour and break the eggs into it, then whisk them into the flour, taking in all the flour from around the edges. Now gradually whisk in the milk and the water. The mixture should be smooth and have the consistency of single cream. Stir in the vanilla extract and the 4 tablespoons of melted butter.

3. Melt a little of the butter for cooking the pancakes in a frying pan over a medium heat. When it is sizzling, add a ladleful of pancake batter to the hot pan. Swirl the mixture around the pan and leave to cook for 2–3 minutes, then turn it over and cook the other side for another 2–3 minutes. Slide the finished pancake on to a warm plate, set it aside to keep warm and repeat with the rest of the mixture. Serve the pancakes with the rum butter.

Ingredients

For the rum butter:
735 g light soft brown sugar
375 g slightly salted butter
50 ml dark rum
little freshly grated nutmeg

For the pancakes:
220 g plain flour
pinch of salt
4 large eggs
400 ml milk, mixed with 150 ml water, or snow
2 tsp vanilla extract
4 tbsp melted butter
50 g butter, for cooking the pancakes

Servings: Makes 20–22 pancakes using an 18 cm pan
Level of difficulty: Easy
Preparation time: 25 minutes, plus 1–2 hours chilling for the rum butter
Cooking time: 15 minutes

The rum butter is delicious – slightly spicy – and this is an easy, spontaneous dish.
Paul

WINNER

SWEET POTATO PUDDING
BY PANCY PATTERSON

I was born in the Jamaican parish of St Ann, the garden parish of Jamaica, and I grew up surrounded by bananas, tangerines and guavas; there was a lot of home-grown food. I came to the UK in 1961, when I was 17. I live in Leeds and help run the Leeds Jamaica Society, which helps young people connect to their Caribbean culture. My grandmother taught me to cook – outside, on a fire – I learned from watching and the recipes became embedded in my mind. She also used to teach me nursery rhymes if I helped!

Ingredients

115 g plain white flour
1 tsp ground mixed spice
1–1½ tsp freshly grated nutmeg
1 tsp salt
900 g Jamaican white-fleshed sweet
   potatoes, peeled and grated
350 g brown sugar
225 g dried fruit: sultanas, raisins
   or currants
400 g can of coconut milk
2 tsp vanilla extract
2 tbsp sugar, optional

1. Preheat the oven to 180°C / gas 4, and grease a 20 cm springform round cake tin. Put the flour, mixed spice, nutmeg and salt into a large mixing bowl and stir in the sweet potatoes. Then add the brown sugar, dried fruit, coconut milk and vanilla extract. Mix everything together really well and then allow the mixture to stand for 1 minute.

2. Pour the mixture into the greased tin and sprinkle it with the sugar if you wish. Bake the pudding for 40–60 minutes until it is firm to the touch, then remove it from the oven and allow it to stand for 30 minutes before serving.

Servings: 6–8
Level of difficulty: Easy
Preparation time: 20 minutes, plus 30
minutes standing once cooked
Cooking time: About 50 minutes

This Jamaican favourite is so moreish and, for me, it's really unusual.
Antony

ANTONY'S CHOICE

HUNTING PUDDING
BY IRENE DUNN

1. Soak the sultanas in the orange juice for 2 hours, and butter an 850 ml pudding basin. Sift the flour into a mixing bowl and stir in the shredded suet and sugar. Add the cinnamon, nutmeg and the orange zest; stir in the soaked sultanas and juice. Beat in the eggs, and the brandy if you're using it.

2. Pour the mixture into the prepared pudding basin. Cover it with a double layer of greaseproof paper, making a folded pleat in the middle to allow for expansion. Tie the paper in place with string, and cover this with foil, also with a pleat across the centre.

3. Place the basin in a steamer basket set over boiling water. Cover and steam for 1 hour 30 minutes–2 hours until the pudding is firm to the touch; check the water level now and again to make sure the pan doesn't burn dry. Serve with custard or double cream.

Ingredients

225 g sultanas
finely grated zest and juice of
  1 large orange
115 g self-raising white flour
115 g shredded suet
115 g dark soft brown sugar
½ tsp ground cinnamon
½ tsp freshly grated nutmeg
2 eggs, beaten
splash of brandy – optional
custard or double cream, to serve

This is a very old, traditional pudding, and you really get the spices coming through.
Antony

Servings: 4
Level of difficulty: Easy
Preparation time: 20 minutes,
plus 2 hours soaking
Cooking time: Up to 2 hours

WINNER

FRUIT SLAB
BY MARGARET BARNES

I'm delighted to have been involved with the People's Cookbook, as I was very keen to share this recipe as a tribute to my mother, who died recently. She was a fantastic baker, and this dish uses her (formerly!) secret recipe for pastry. I do a lot of baking myself – I'm a fundraiser for the Fire Service Benevolent Fund and love making delicious cakes and biscuits as treats for the brave men and women who risk their lives for other people.

1. To prepare the pastry, sift the flour and salt into a bowl. Using your fingertips, lightly rub the margarine and butter into the flour until the mixture resembles breadcrumbs. Stir in the sugar and then add the beaten egg, mixing until the ingredients bind together to make a soft dough. Knead the dough until smooth, then put it in a polythene food bag and leave it to rest in the fridge for 20–30 minutes.

2. To make the filling, put the currants, mixed spice and sugar in a large pan and add enough cold water to just cover the fruit. Bring the mixture to the boil and simmer for no more than 5 minutes, then remove the pan from the heat. Gradually add the custard paste, stirring until the fruit mixture has thickened slightly (bear in mind that it will thicken even more when cold).

3. Preheat the oven to 170°C / gas 3. Grease a 30 x 18 cm Swiss roll tin and line it with non-stick baking paper. Divide the pastry in half. Roll out one portion of pastry on a lightly floured surface and use it to line the prepared tin, pressing the pastry over the base and up the sides. Lightly brush the top edges with water.

4. Spoon the fruit mixture into the pastry case, spreading it evenly and packing it in well. Roll out the remaining pastry into a rectangle just slightly larger than the tin, then put this sheet of pastry over the filling and pat it down lightly. Using a sharp knife, trim away any excess pastry, crimp the edges, and cut 2 slits in the middle of the top of the pie. Bake it in the oven for 50–60 minutes until the pastry is cooked and golden.

5. Take it out of the oven and sprinkle it with caster sugar or vanilla sugar while still hot. Leave it to cool and serve warm or cold, in slices.

Cook's note: to make vanilla sugar, simply store one or two vanilla pods in a container of caster sugar, leaving the pod in the sugar for at least a week before use and stirring it occasionally.

Ingredients
For the pastry:
750 g plain white flour, plus extra
    for dusting
pinch of salt
225 g margarine or butter
250 g butter (at room temperature),
    plus extra for greasing
250 g caster sugar, plus extra
    for sprinkling
1 egg, beaten

For the filling:
550 g currants
1 heaped tsp ground mixed spice
4 heaped tsp granulated sugar
2 heaped tsp custard powder, mixed
    with a little cold water to make a fairly
    thick, smooth paste

caster or vanilla sugar, to serve

Servings: 6–10
Level of difficulty: Intermediate
Preparation time: 35 minutes, plus 20–30
minutes chilling time
Cooking time: 1 hour–1 hour 10 minutes

A powerful number, this one, with loads of impact.
It would be just perfect with a nice cup of tea.
Antony

WINNER

QUEEN OF PUDDINGS
BY ANN MULLER

I run a pastry shop on the Lizard in Cornwall and got my passion for traditional British food – and especially Cornish dishes – from my mother, Hetty. She fed the family hearty food and homely desserts like this pudding, which was handy because it used any stale bread left at the end of the week. This is one of her recipes, though it actually came from my grandmother, who brought it back from London where she had been in service.

Ingredients

For the base:
55 g white breadcrumbs
300 ml milk
2 egg yolks
3 tbsp red jam (raspberry, strawberry or plum), warmed

For the meringue:
2 egg whites
115 g caster sugar

1. Preheat the oven to 180°C / gas 4. Butter a 600 ml ovenproof serving dish and spread the breadcrumbs over the base. Combine the milk and the egg yolks and then pour this mixture over the breadcrumbs. Allow it to stand for 5 minutes and then put the dish in the oven and bake for 25 minutes until the base of the pudding has set – test for this by pressing it gently with your finger. Remove the dish from the oven once it is ready and reduce the oven temperature to 170°C / gas 3. Leave the pudding to cool slightly then spread the warmed jam over the top.

2. Make the meringue for the topping. Whisk the egg whites until stiff, then gently fold in the caster sugar. Pile the meringue on top of the pudding and return the dish to the oven for about 15 minutes until the meringue is light gold and set.

I love it when you see the layers here; so simple but beautiful – Queen of Puddings should come back to popularity. Cook this dish!
Paul

Servings: 2–4
Level of difficulty: Intermediate
Preparation time: 20 minutes
Cooking time: About 40 minutes

WINNER

FLOSSIE'S TRIFLE
BY FLOSSIE SQUIRES

I'm 83 and this reminds me of my childhood growing up on the farm, when my mother used to make it for parties and harvest suppers. She didn't actually teach me, I just learned by watching; she said that if we children cooked, we used too many ingredients. Now my cousin Derek says I put too much sherry in trifle, but I think it's fine; just put in the amount that suits you. I love cooking and often cook to thank people for doing odd jobs.

1. Start by preparing the jellies. Place the raspberry jelly cubes in a heatproof jug and add 150 ml of boiling water, stirring until the jelly is dissolved. Add enough cold water to the dissolved jelly to make it up to 430 ml. Repeat the same procedure with the lemon jelly cubes in a separate heatproof jug.

2. Drain the pears, reserving the juice. Stir the pear juice and lemon juice into the dissolved lemon jelly, then stir in one-quarter of the dissolved raspberry jelly, to give it some colour. Keep the remaining raspberry jelly for decoration (pour it into a bowl and chill it in the fridge until set). Reserve 2 pear halves and a few raspberries for decoration as well, then slice the remaining pears and put them in a deep glass bowl with most of the raspberries. Pour the lemon jelly over the fruit and chill until set.

3. Place the trifle sponge cakes over the jelly, then drizzle some sherry over the top. Pour a little of the hot custard over the sponge cakes but leave the remaining custard to cool before pouring it evenly over the sponge cakes too. Chill the trifle again at this stage, if desired.

4. Decorate the trifle with the reserved raspberry jelly, pear halves and raspberries. One suggestion for the decoration is to put a pear half, with a few raspberries in the hollow of the pear, in the centre of the trifle. Place slices of the remaining pear and the rest of the raspberries around this central decoration. Roughly chop the reserved set raspberry jelly and sprinkle the pieces around the edge of the trifle. Serve with clotted cream.

Ingredients
135 g packet of raspberry jelly,
   broken into cubes
135 g packet of lemon jelly, broken
   into cubes
415 g can of pear halves in fruit juice
juice of ½ lemon
450 g raspberries (fresh, if possible)
6 trifle sponge cakes
sherry, to taste
575 ml instant custard
   (made using 100g instant custard
   powder and boiling water)
clotted cream to serve

Servings: 6
Level of difficulty: Easy
Preparation time: 35 minutes,
plus chilling and setting times

A classic kiddie trifle – well, except for the sherry! – so how could Flossie not win?
Antony

PAVLOVA (TWO WAYS)

BY JANE JOHNS

1. Preheat the oven to 200°C / gas 6 and line 2 baking trays with baking parchment. Whisk the egg whites at high speed until they are stiff, preferably using an electric mixer. Then gradually whisk in the sugar in a thin stream and continue whisking at a low speed until all the sugar has been fully mixed in. Then whisk in the cornflour, vinegar and vanilla.

2. Using a large spoon, palette knife or piping bag, put half the meringue mixture on to the baking parchment on the first baking tray, making a circle about 20 cm across. Create a lip at the edge so that it is slightly higher than the base. Then make another circle, using the rest of the mixture, on the second baking tray – try to keep the sizes as similar as possible. Place the baking trays in the oven and immediately lower the temperature to 110°C / gas ¼, or the lowest setting on your oven. Cook the pavlovas for 1–2 hours until they are firm and crisp. Take them out of the oven and leave them to cool. Once they are cold, carefully remove the baking parchment and put them on serving plates.

3. For the filling, fold the lemon curd gently into the whipped cream and pile it over the Pavlova cases. Top with either raspberries or strawberries, for the summer filling, or glacé cherries and angelica, for the winter filling.

Ingredients
6 egg whites
350 g caster sugar
2 tsp cornflour
2 tsp white wine vinegar
1 tsp vanilla extract

For the summer filling:
4 tbsp lemon curd
275 ml whipped cream
350 g fresh raspberries or strawberries

For the winter filling:
4 tbsp lemon curd
275 ml whipped cream
25 g glacé cherries, halved
2 tsp angelica, chopped

A lovely thing; nice and craggy. And varying the ingredients with the seasons – excellent.
Antony

Servings: Makes 2 Pavlovas
Level of difficulty: Intermediate
Preparation time: 20 minutes
Cooking time: Up to 2 hours

WINNER

PASSION FRUIT FRIDGE TART WITH COULIS
BY CAROL MAXWELL

I was born in Scotland, but lived there for only nine weeks as my family moved to South Africa. We went because my father, a professional footballer in the 1960s with Falkirk and Celtic, transferred to Hellenic, a South African team. This recipe reminds me of sunny days there – I came back to the UK to work and my parents returned too – and is a bit of a tribute to my father. My parents were very keen gardeners and always grew passion fruit, and we used to get inventive with recipes. This is perfect as a post-barbeque dessert.

1. For the tart, start by making the lemon jelly, but use half the quantity of water specified on the packet, then set aside to cool. While it is cooling, make the tart base by melting the butter in a saucepan and stirring in the crushed biscuits. Mix them thoroughly, then tip into 8 individual tart tins with removable bases or a 20 x 30 cm shallow pie dish. Press the mixture down to cover the base in an even layer and put the dish in the fridge to chill.

2. Beat the evaporated milk and add the sugar gradually, still beating as you go. Then stir in the passion fruit pulp and, finally, the cooled lemon jelly. Pour this mixture over the chilled biscuit base and put the dish back in the fridge to set, which will take approximately 1–2 hours.

3. Make the coulis once the dish is in the fridge, as this also needs to cool. Scrape out the flesh from the 6 passion fruit and (if necessary) make the quantity up to 200 ml with cold water. Pour this into a small saucepan along with the sugar and scrape in the seeds from the vanilla pod. Stir the mixture over a low heat until the sugar has dissolved, then increase the heat slightly and simmer, stirring frequently, until it is reduced by about half, to 125 ml. Pour the coulis into a bowl, leave it to cool and then chill it until you are ready to serve the tart. Unmould the individual tart or slice a large one, and accompany each piece with a little pool of coulis.

Ingredients
For the tart:
135 g packet of lemon jelly
100 g butter
250 g ginger biscuits (or digestives); crushed
500 ml sweetened evaporated milk, chilled
125 ml caster sugar
125 ml passion fruit pulp from approx 5 passion fruit, after sieveing

For the coulis:
6 passion fruit
125 ml caster sugar
½ a vanilla pod, split lengthwise

Servings: 8
Level of difficulty: Easy
Preparation time: 30 minutes, plus 2 hours chilling
Cooking time: 10 minutes

This is simple but satisfying, and the passion fruit cuts through the richness. Paul

WINNER

KONAFA

BY FATIMA MUGANZI

I converted to Islam eight years ago, and an essential part of Muslim culture is the enjoyment of feeding people and eating together. I love the creative side of cooking – I'm no good at other forms of art – and love teaching my four stepchildren to cook too. This is a very traditional Middle Eastern dessert; each country has its own version, but I learned this one when I was living with friends in Cairo. I always make it for the family during Ramadan, as a treat. They fast during the day and I like to make them something special for afterwards.

Ingredients

For the syrup:
225 g caster sugar
100 ml water
4 tsp clear honey
2–3 tbsp lime juice
2–3 tbsp rose water
1 tsp ground cinnamon,
   or 3 cm cinnamon stick
pinch of saffron strands

For the pastry:
400 g konafa
   (sweet Arabic pastry; see cook's note)
handful of mixed nuts and dried fruit,
   chopped
200 g butter, melted

Greek yogurt or ice cream, to serve

1. Make the syrup by heating the sugar, water, honey, lime juice (to taste), rose water (to taste), cinnamon and saffron in a pan over a low heat. Simmer for 10–15 minutes until the syrup starts to thicken, and then remove the pan from the heat and leave to cool. Preheat the oven to 170°C / gas 3.

2. Spread out the konafa and separate it as much as possible; place half evenly in an ovenproof serving dish. Sprinkle the chopped nuts and fruit over the pastry, then place the remaining konafa on top. Pour the melted butter over it. Bake for 45 minutes, then increase the oven temperature to 230°C / gas 8 and continue cooking for a further 10–15 minutes until the konafa is golden. Remove it from the oven and pour over the cold syrup. Serve hot or cold with Greek yogurt or ice cream.

Cook's note: You can find packets of konafa pastry in the chiller cabinets of Middle Eastern and Greek food shops. It looks like thin strands of vermicelli or shredded wheat.

Cooking konafa is fascinating and it's nice and crunchy, even with that lovely syrup on it.
Antony

Servings: 10
Level of difficulty: Intermediate
Preparation time: 25 minutes
Cooking time: About 1 hour 15 minutes

BLACK FOREST GATEAU
BY NIGEL KIRKUP

1. Preheat the oven to 180°C / gas 4, and grease and flour two 20 cm sandwich cake tins. Beat the butter and caster sugar together in a large bowl until pale and fluffy, then add the eggs, a little at a time, beating well between each addition.

2. Sieve the flour and cocoa into the bowl and fold them in gently until everything is fully combined. Divide the mixture between the 2 prepared cake tins and bake for about 25 minutes, until the cakes spring back to the touch and a skewer inserted into the centre comes out clean. Leave them to cool for a few minutes in the tins before turning them out and letting them cool completely on a wire rack.

3. Prepare the filling. Stir the arrowroot into a little of the juice from the cherries, then add it to the remaining juice. Put the cherry juice into a small pan and warm it over a gentle heat until the sauce thickens, then leave it to cool. Beat the cream until it forms soft peaks, and coarsely grate 60 g of the chocolate; set aside.

4. Melt the remaining chocolate in a bowl over a pan of simmering water (or in the microwave, but keep a close eye on it). Once it has melted completely, remove the bowl from the heat and beat the egg yolks into the chocolate. Beat the egg whites until stiff, then beat 1 tablespoon of them into the melted chocolate. Beat in 1 tablespoon of the cream as well, to loosen the mixture, before folding in the remaining egg whites.

5. Slice the cooled cakes in half horizontally, sprinkle a little of the optional kirsch on to each one and sandwich them together with the chocolate mixture. Pipe or spoon a 4 cm band of cream around the top of one of the two cakes and fill the 'cavity' with the cherries (reserving about 8 for decoration). Pour the thickened juice over them and then gently place the other cake on top. Cover the whole cake, top and side, with a layer of cream and coat the side with the grated chocolate until it is speckled with chocolate shavings. Pipe rosettes of cream around the top and top each alternative one with a cherry. Fill the centre of the circle with more grated chocolate. Cut into slices to serve.

Ingredients
225 g unsalted butter, softened
225 g caster sugar
4 large eggs, lightly beaten
200 g self-raising white flour
25 g cocoa

For the filling:
2 heaped tsp arrowroot
400g can of pitted morello cherries, drained, juice reserved
1 litre double cream, lightly whipped
175 g dark chocolate, minimum 70% cocoa solids
2 eggs, separated
little kirsch, optional

This is just so impressive – a spectacular cake which the kids will love (though maybe without the kirsch!).
Paul

Servings: 8–10
Level of difficulty: Intermediate
Preparation time: 50 minutes
Cooking time: About 30 minutes

ANTONY'S CHOICE

WHITE CHOCOLATE AND RASPBERRY CHEESECAKE
BY CLARE CLOUTING

1. Combine the crushed digestives and gingernuts with the melted butter, and press the mixture into the base of a 23 cm springform cake tin.

2. Put the white chocolate, butter and vanilla pod in a heatproof bowl and set over a pan of simmering (not boiling) water until the chocolate and butter have melted. Leave the mixture to cool slightly. In another bowl, mix together the cream cheese, sugar and whipping cream until you have a smooth consistency. Remove the vanilla pod from the white chocolate mixture and set it aside; it can be used again if you rinse and dry it. Stir the chocolate into the cream cheese mixture and then gently stir in the raspberries; be careful not to crush them.

3. Spoon the mixture on top of the biscuit base and chill the cheesecake overnight. When you are ready to serve, remove it carefully from the tin. Slice into wedges and serve with extra raspberries.

Ingredients

For the biscuit base:
75 g digestive biscuits, crushed
75 g gingernut biscuits, crushed
75 g butter, melted

For the filling:
500 g white chocolate,
   broken into pieces
65 g butter
½ vanilla pod
500 g cream cheese
50 g caster sugar
180 ml whipping cream
1 punnet fresh raspberries,
   plus a few more to serve

Servings: 6
Level of difficulty: Easy
Preparation time: 20 minutes,
plus 8–24 hours chilling.

A great cheesecake which doesn't involve the use of gelatine – it just sets in the fridge. Definitely a bonus.
Antony

WINNER

MALVA PUDDING

BY MARIANNE WILLIAMS

I live in Somerset, in a house often credited with being the home of English cottage gardening, and I like to cook with produce from the garden whenever I can. I'm really passionate about good, hearty food – nothing too fancy – and I love baking; I started a tea room a few years ago. I'm also passionate about teaching my three young daughters to cook in the way that I was taught by my own mother. This recipe came from my grandmother – it's a South African variation on sticky toffee pudding, and it's definitely not for slimmers!

Ingredients

225 g caster sugar
1 egg
1 tbsp apricot jam
115 g self-raising white flour
1 tbsp bicarbonate of soda
pinch of salt
200 ml semi-skimmed milk
1 tbsp butter, melted
1 tbsp white wine vinegar

For the sauce:
200 ml single cream
175 g butter
225 g caster sugar
100 ml hot water

1. Preheat the oven to 200°C / gas 6 and grease a 500 ml pudding bowl.

2. Using a large mixing bowl, beat the sugar, egg and apricot jam together with an electric whisk until pale in colour. Sieve the flour, bicarbonate of soda and pinch of salt into another bowl. Leave on one side.

3. Stir 100 ml of the milk into the sugar, egg and jam mixture and blend in well. Then fold in half of the sieved flour mixture, followed by the remaining milk and then the rest of the flour. Fold in the melted butter and vinegar. Pour the mixture into the greased pudding bowl and cover with foil. Bake for 45–60 minutes until the pudding is firm to the touch and browned.

4. Make the sauce when the pudding is nearly ready. Put the single cream, butter, caster sugar and hot water in a pan and heat gently until the sugar has dissolved. Bring this to the boil. Remove the pudding from the oven, turn it out of the bowl and pour the sauce over. Leave it to stand for several minutes before serving, so that the pudding can absorb the sauce.

One big, irresistible, delicious pudding with such a simple sauce. It's very sensuous.
Paul

Servings: 6–8
Level of difficulty: Easy
Preparation time: 30 minutes
Cooking time: About 1 hour 10 minutes

ANTONY'S CHOICE

TIRAMISU

BY NATALIA POPOVA

1. Start by making the cake. Preheat the oven to 200°C / gas 6, and grease and line a 33 x 23 cm Swiss roll tin and set it to one side. Put the butter, sugar, flour and beaten eggs in a bowl and beat them together for 1–2 minutes, or until smooth and glossy. Transfer the mixture to the prepared tin and level the surface. Bake it for 15–20 minutes or until risen, golden brown and just firm to the touch. Turn it out on to a wire rack and leave it to cool.

2. Now prepare the mascarpone cheese mixture. Whisk the egg whites in a bowl until they form stiff peaks, then set them aside. Put the egg yolks in a separate bowl with the icing sugar and beat them together until they are evenly blended and creamy. Add the mascarpone and Irish cream liqueur and stir, mixing everything together well. Then gently fold in the whisked egg whites until they are evenly incorporated.

3. You can either use individual clear serving dishes or one large one for this dish. Pour the coffee into a shallow dish and cut circles out of the cold cake using a glass. Dip each cake circle in the cold coffee, then place one cake circle in the base of each individual serving bowl, or place a layer of cake circles in the base of the large serving dish. Spoon a layer of the mascarpone mixture over the cake. Repeat these layers until you have used up all the ingredients, ending with a layer of mascarpone mixture. Sift cocoa powder liberally all over the top, cover and chill for at least 2 hours before serving.

Ingredients

For the cake:
200 g butter, softened
200 g caster sugar
200 g self-raising white flour, sifted
4 eggs, beaten

For the mascarpone mixture:
4 eggs, separated
100 g icing sugar
500 g mascarpone
100 ml Irish cream liqueur or
  coffee-flavoured liqueur
100 ml cold strong black coffee
cocoa powder, for sprinkling

It's a shame this didn't win because it deserved to;
I love a good tiramisu.
Antony

Servings: 4–6
Level of difficulty: Intermediate
Preparation time: 35 minutes, plus cooling
and chilling time
Cooking time: 15–20 minutes

WINNER

CLOOTIE DUMPLING
BY HAZEL MACFADZEAN

I grew up on a farm outside Perth with three older brothers. My mother's a great cook, and we all brought our friends home – she fed everyone. She taught me to cook, especially very traditional dishes, but she's a hard act to follow so I tend to make different things to avoid comparisons! This is a classic Scottish dish, and everyone has their own version. In our family it was always made for special occasions, like birthdays (when it has a coin hidden inside). If we're having clootie dumpling it means the whole family will be together.

1. Make the dumpling. Using a large mixing bowl, rub the butter into the flour until the mixture resembles breadcrumbs. Add the breadcrumbs, caster sugar, dried fruit, bicarbonate of soda, cinnamon and mixed spice and stir to combine. Lightly beat the egg with the milk and add this to the mixture. Stir well, bringing everything together to form a firm dough.

2. Put a large cotton cloth in a heatproof bowl, pour boiling water over it and wring it out as tightly as possible – wear rubber gloves for this. Spread the cloth out on the work surface and coat the uppermost surface with plain flour. Place the dumpling mixture in the centre of the cloth, then bring the edges of the cloth up around the dumpling and secure them tightly with a piece of string. Don't wrap the cloth too tightly around the dumpling, as it will expand on cooking.

3. Put a heatproof plate in the bottom of a large saucepan. Place the cloth-wrapped dumpling on the plate and then fill the pan with boiling water so that the water comes 5 cm above the top of the dumpling. Simmer it gently for about 3 hours. Ensure that the dumpling is covered with water at all times, topping it up regularly with more boiling water as required. After the dumpling has been cooking for 2 hours, turn it over.

4. Preheat the oven to 140°C/gas 1. Remove the pan from the heat and lift the dumpling out. Undo the string and tip the dumpling out of the cloth on to an ovenproof plate. Bake it in the oven for about 15 minutes to crisp up the outside.

5. While it is baking, make the custard. Warm the milk and cream together in a pan over a low heat until just below boiling point, then remove the pan from the heat. Beat the egg yolks, sugar and cornflour together in a large bowl until the egg yolks turn pale, then add a little of the hot milk and cream. Mix this in well before gradually adding the remainder. Pour the custard into a clean pan and cook it over a low heat, stirring constantly until it thickens enough to coat the back of a spoon – take care not to let it boil or it will curdle.

6. Take the clootie dumpling out of the oven, slice, and serve with hot custard.

Ingredients

For the clootie:
200 g chilled butter, diced
350 g plain white flour, plus extra
   for coating
200 g fresh breadcrumbs
175 g caster sugar
175 g sultanas
175 g currants and raisins
½ tsp bicarbonate of soda
½ tsp ground cinnamon
½ tsp ground mixed spice
1 large free-range egg
50 ml full-fat milk

For the egg custard:
300 ml milk
284 ml single cream
5 large free range egg yolks
50 g caster sugar
1 tsp cornflour

Level of difficulty: Intermediate
Preparation time: 30 minutes
Cooking time: About 3 hours 15 minutes

I love this type of hot pudding with custard; it
reminds me of good school dinners!
Paul

PAUL'S CHOICE

VICTORIA SPONGE WITH LEMON CURD
BY HELEN HOSKER

1. Make the lemon curd. Put the lemon zest and juice, eggs, butter and caster sugar in a heatproof bowl. Place this over a pan of simmering water and stir continuously until all the butter has melted – don't let it boil or it will curdle. Continue stirring for about 15 minutes until the mixture is creamy and thick. Strain it through a sieve into a clean jar, and leave to cool before using it in the Victoria sandwich cake. This curd will keep in the fridge for a week or two.

2. For the cake, preheat the oven to 170°C / gas 3, and grease and line two 20 cm sandwich cake tins. Using a mixer, cream the butter and sugar until the mixture is light and fluffy, then add the grated lemon zest. Sift the flour and baking powder into another bowl. Add the eggs to the creamed mixture but do this gradually, a little at a time, and add a tablespoonful of the flour for each egg to stop the mixture curdling. Beat it well after each addition. Using a metal spoon, gently fold in the remaining flour and baking powder, and then fold in as much lemon juice as you need to give a soft, dropping consistency.

3. Spoon the mixture into the prepared tins and level the surface with a knife. Bake the cakes in the centre of the oven for about 25 minutes. You can tell when the cakes are cooked because they should shrink slightly away from the sides of the tins and the tops will feel springy to the touch. Remove them from the oven and leave them to cool in their tins for 5 minutes, then turn them out onto a wire rack to finish cooling.

4. Once they are cold, spread with a generous layer of lemon curd and sandwich the 2 cakes together. Sprinkle the top with icing or caster sugar before serving.

Ingredients

For the lemon curd:
finely grated zest and juice of 2
  unwaxed lemons
2 eggs, lightly beaten
50 g unsalted butter
175 g caster sugar

For the cake:
225 g butter, softened
225 g golden caster sugar
finely grated zest of 1 unwaxed lemon
225 g self-raising white flour
1 tsp baking powder
4 eggs, lightly beaten
4 tbsp lemon juice
icing sugar or caster sugar, to decorate

Servings: Makes 1 x 20 cm sandwich cake
Level of difficulty: Easy
Preparation time: 20 minutes
Cooking time: 40 minutes

A baking staple with a slant: zingy lemon curd, which is a really simple thing to make.
Paul

WINNER

CHRISTMAS CAKE WITH MARMALADE
BY ANN WAY

I've always loved cooking and write recipes for my local church magazine. This recipe actually helped me woo my husband! After we first met, I sent him a slice of cake and a jar of my marmalade, and he invited me out to the theatre. Eleven meetings later we were engaged! We've now been married for 47 years, and every year I've made my Christmas Cake and marmalade. Adding marmalade to the cake gives it an extra zing, and I also like to add extra brandy while the cake rests before Christmas; I stick a skewer in the bottom and drizzle it in.

Ingredients

115 g mixed peel
115 g glacé cherries, chopped
450 g currants
225 g sultanas
225 g seedless raisins
350 g plain flour, sifted
1 tbsp black treacle, warmed
2 tbsp brandy
5 large eggs, beaten
280 g butter
280 g dark muscovado sugar
1 tsp ground mixed spice
½ nutmeg, freshly grated
1 tsp ground cinnamon
½ tsp salt
115 g blanched almonds, finely chopped
finely grated zest of 1 lemon
1 tbsp Seville orange marmalade

1. Preheat the oven to 150°C / gas 2. Lightly grease either a 23 cm round cake tin or a 20 cm square one, and line the base and sides with brown paper. Then cut greaseproof paper to the same size as the brown paper and line the inside of the tin – cut 1 cm slits upwards at the bottom of the side pieces, so they will lie flat under the base papers. Allow enough paper to stand at least 5 cm above the rim of the tin. Fit a cover of brown paper around the outside to also come 5 cm above the edge of the tin and secure this with string.

2. Place all the fruit in a large bowl and add a tablespoon of flour from the measured quantity; stir everything together to lightly coat the fruit in flour. In another bowl mix the treacle with the brandy, and then stir this into the beaten eggs.

3. Cream the butter and sugar in a large mixing bowl until soft and creamy. Carefully add the egg mixture alternately with a spoonful of the sieved flour (this stops it curdling). Gradually stir in the rest of the flour, the mixed spice, nutmeg, cinnamon and the salt until well mixed. Add the fruit mixture, the almonds, lemon zest and marmalade and stir well until the fruit is evenly distributed.

4. Spoon the mixture into the prepared cake tin and bake for 1 hour 30 minutes. Reduce the oven temperature to 140°C / gas 1 and cook for another 1 hour 30 minutes to 2 hours, until cooked. To test the cake, press the top firmly. If it feels firm, take it out of the oven and listen; if there is a slight humming noise it needs more cooking. Turn the cake out once it is done and cool it on a wire rack. Wrap it in greaseproof paper when it is cold and store it in an airtight tin, for a few weeks, until you are ready to decorate it.

Servings: Makes one 23 cm round or 20 cm square cake
Level of difficulty: Intermediate
Preparation time: 30 minutes
Cooking time: 3 hours 30 minutes

A fab cake – lots of lovely fruit and then the little bit of marmalade. And it isn't remotely heavy, either.
Antony

WINNER

APRICOT BRIOCHE DELIGHT
BY MALCOLM ARCHER

I grew up with fairly unadventurous cooking but my eyes were opened while I was at Cambridge University on an Organ Scholarship. As a Scholar, I dined with the college fellows and they enjoyed some wonderful, interesting meals which really kick-started my love of food and opened my mind. I find cooking very therapeutic; it helps me wind down after work. I was given the recipe for this ice cream by a very good friend – and fine musician – Alan Harwood. He died a few years ago, but both my wife and I remember him with great affection.

Ingredients

For the apricot and amaretti ice cream:
350 g good quality apricot jam
2 tbsp lemon juice
284 ml double cream
280 g amaretti biscuits, crumbled

For the apricot brioche:
1 egg
2 tbsp caster sugar
250 g mascarpone cheese
225 g brioche, cut into 1 cm slices
2 x 400 g cans of apricot halves, drained
4 tbsp demerara sugar
icing sugar, for dusting

1. Make the apricot and amaretti ice cream in advance. Combine the apricot jam with the lemon juice. Very lightly whip the cream and fold it into the jam, then gently fold in the amaretti biscuits. Spoon the ice cream mixture into a freezer container and freeze it for 1 hour, then stir well to break up the ice crystals. Repeat this 3 or 4 times until the mixture is nearly frozen, then leave it to freeze completely.

2. For the apricot brioche, grease a 28 cm shallow ovenproof dish and preheat the oven to 180°C / gas 4. Whisk the egg and sugar together in a bowl until the mixture is pale and creamy, then add the mascarpone and whisk it again until smooth. Arrange the brioche slices in the dish as neatly as possible in a single layer, and spread the mascarpone mixture over the slices to about 1 cm from the edge (it spreads during baking). Finally, arrange the apricot halves neatly in circles over the top, going right to the edge of the dish. Sprinkle them with the demerara sugar.

3. Bake for 30–35 minutes until the mascarpone custard is set and golden. Leave the ice cream to soften for about 20 minutes in the fridge, and serve with the hot pudding.

Servings: 4–6
Level of difficulty: Easy
Preparation time: 30 minutes, plus 4–6 hours freezing
Cooking time: 35 minutes

I was a bit unsure about this, but wow, what a taste!
Antony

INDEX

INDEX

START CHANGING YOUR LIFE
IN FIVE MINUTES...

With the **52 Brilliant Ideas** series you can enhance your existing skills or knowledge with negligible investment of time or money and can substantially improve your performance or know-how of a subject over the course of a year. Or day. Or month. The choice is yours. With the help of our expert authors you can achieve your goals and live your life on your own terms – remember, *one brilliant idea can change your life.*

Look gorgeous always
Linda Bird

Stress proof your life
Elisabeth Wilson

Save the planet
Natalia Marshall

Transform your life
Penny Ferguson

Raising teenagers
Lynn Huggins-Cooper

Defeat depression
Dr Sabina Dosani

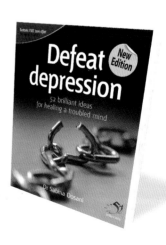

Healthy cooking for children
Mandy Francis

Cultivate a cool career
Ken Langdon

Writing bestselling children's books
Alexander Gordon Smith

The Manly Man Manual
Steve Shipside

Goddess
Elisabeth Wilson

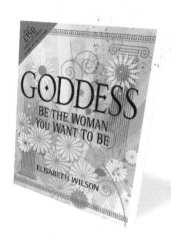

Slow down
Elisabeth Wilson

Visit our website at **www.infideas.com** to see our full range of inspirational titles.

Join our mailing list at **www.infideas.com** and be entered into our monthly prize draw to win 3 books of your choice, worth over £35, from our bestselling **52 Brilliant Ideas** series. In addition, the first 100 readers to email thepeoplescookbook@infideas.com with their name, address and telephone number will win a copy of one of our top humour titles, *Getting away with it: Short cuts to the things you don't really deserve.*

Start changing your life in five minutes… with the **52 Brilliant Ideas** series.

www.infideas.com

LIMITED STOCKS – ORDER TODAY

☑ **YES,** please send **The Superb Spanish Reds Case** for just £55.98 (£49.99 plus £5.99 p&p)

Phone – **0870 066 5686** or order online at www.uktvwineclub/cookbook or complete this form and return it with your payment to: UKTV Wine Club, FREEPOST (SCE6179), Reading RG7 4ZW.

Title _____ Initials _____ Surname _____

Address _____

_____ Postcode _____

Safe place to leave if out (Please specify somewhere sheltered and out of public view) _____

_____

Daytime Telephone _____ Evening Telephone _____

e-mail address _____

☐ Please tick if you wish to receive special offers from UKTV Wine Club

I enclose payment for the amount indicated made payable to '**UKTV Wine Club**' or please charge my
VISA / MASTERCARD / AMEX / DINERS CLUB / MAESTRO card:

[| | | | | | | | | | | | | | | | | |]

Maestro issue number: [|] Valid date: [| | |] Expiry date: [|]

Signature _____ (I am over 18 years of age) Date _____

Call 0870 066 5686

Weekdays 8am – 11pm   Weekends 8am – 9pm   **QUOTE REF: Cookbook**

or order online at **www.uktvwineclub.co.uk/cookbook**

Terms and Conditions

UKTV Wine Club is committed to ensuring that its services are available to all, and in particular seeks to comply with the provisions of The Disability Discrimination Act.
If you require any assistance please contact the Customer Services Department 0870 066 5686.
Purchasers must be aged 18 years or over. New customers only. Maximum one case (plus 3 free Riojas) per household. Offer only available while stocks last. In the unlikely event of a wine becoming unavailable, a substitute of similar style and of equal or greater value will be supplied. If you are unhappy with any substitutions you receive we will arrange collection at our cost. Max. 7 day UK delivery, excluding Channel Islands, further terms and conditions supplied upon request. Direct Wines will use information about you to make offers based on your wine preferences. This information may be shared with companies within the Direct Wines group and may be combined with data about you from other organisations you deal with to enable you to receive offers, products or services that may interest you, from other companies. If you do not wish to receive further offers then please write or call. Calls from BT landlines to numbers beginning with an 0870 code operated by UKTV Wine Club cost up to 10p per min. The price of calls may vary with other operators. Please check with your operator for exact charges.

Direct Wines Ltd trading as UKTV Wine Club, New Aquitaine House, Exeter Way, Reading RG7 4PL